Homoween

Adult Coloring Book

by

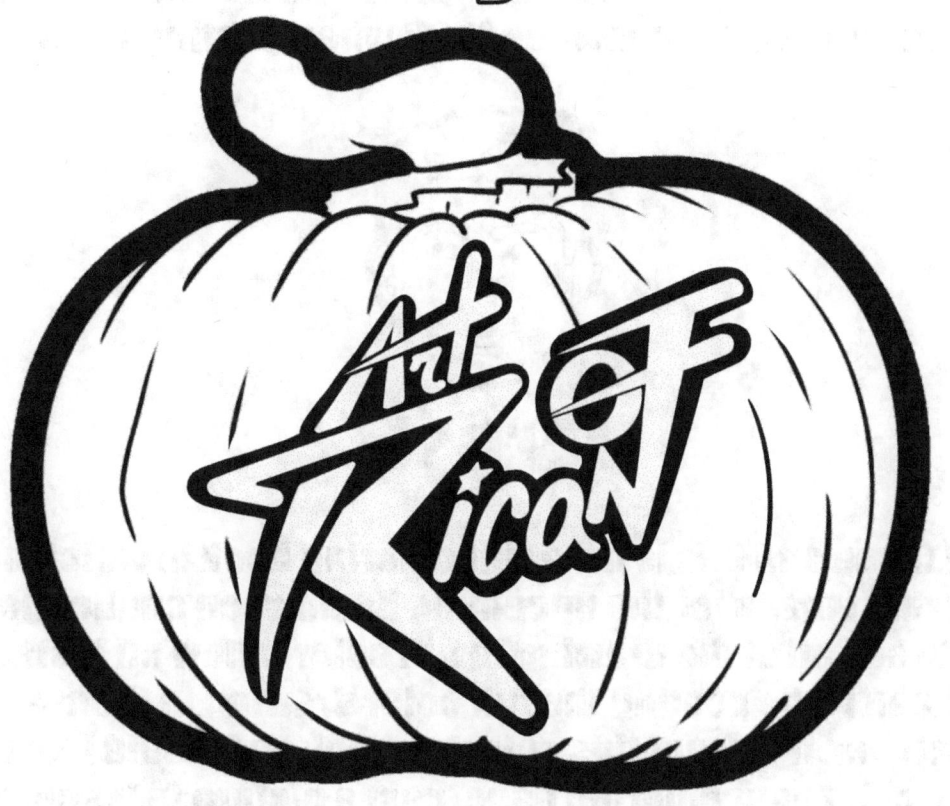

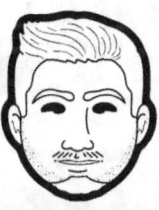

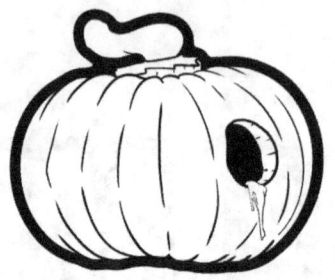

Homoween

Homoween is a online calender art challenge on instagram that starts on the 1st day of October. It's a LGBT art challenge in which y'all artist are welcome to participate and interpreted the daily teams. If your interested in participating follow @Homoweenofficial on Instagram and use #homoween2020 when posting on Instagram.

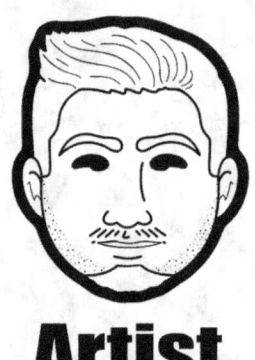

Artist

I'm Art.of.Rican and this is my adult coloring book in which has all of the drawing I made for the upcoming homoween challenge. If you want to see all of the drawing in full color follow mi instagram @Art.of.Rican I'll be posting the full color drawing in their respective days on October. If you get this coloring book and would like too share how you color your coloring page, post a picture in Instagram on @Art.of.rican or Twiter @Art_of_Rican and use the #theartofrican #artofrican. I'll be posting them spooky hunks of your colorings pages on mi Instagram story!

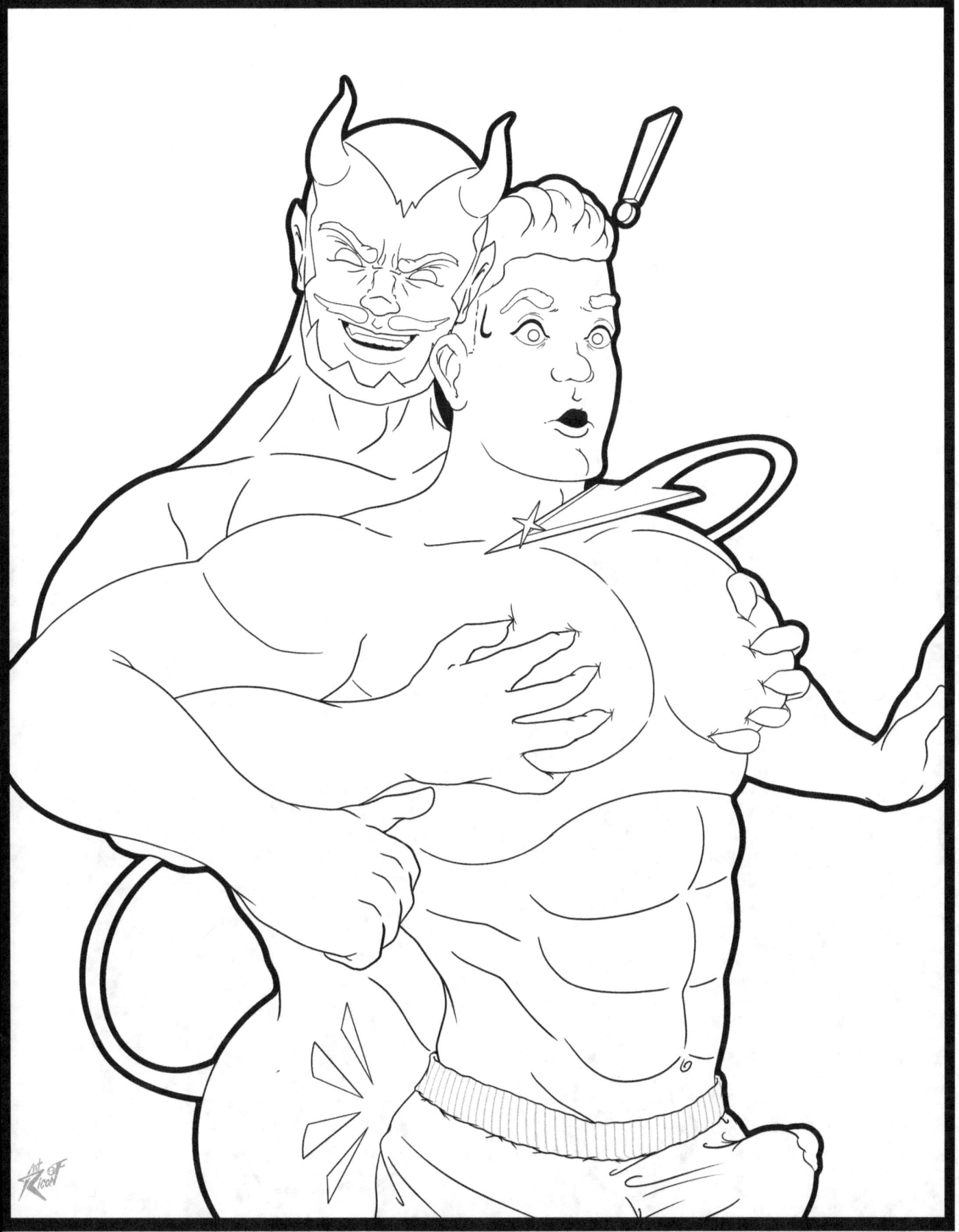

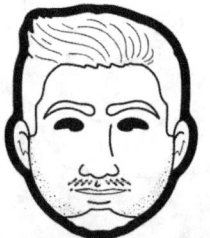 **1**

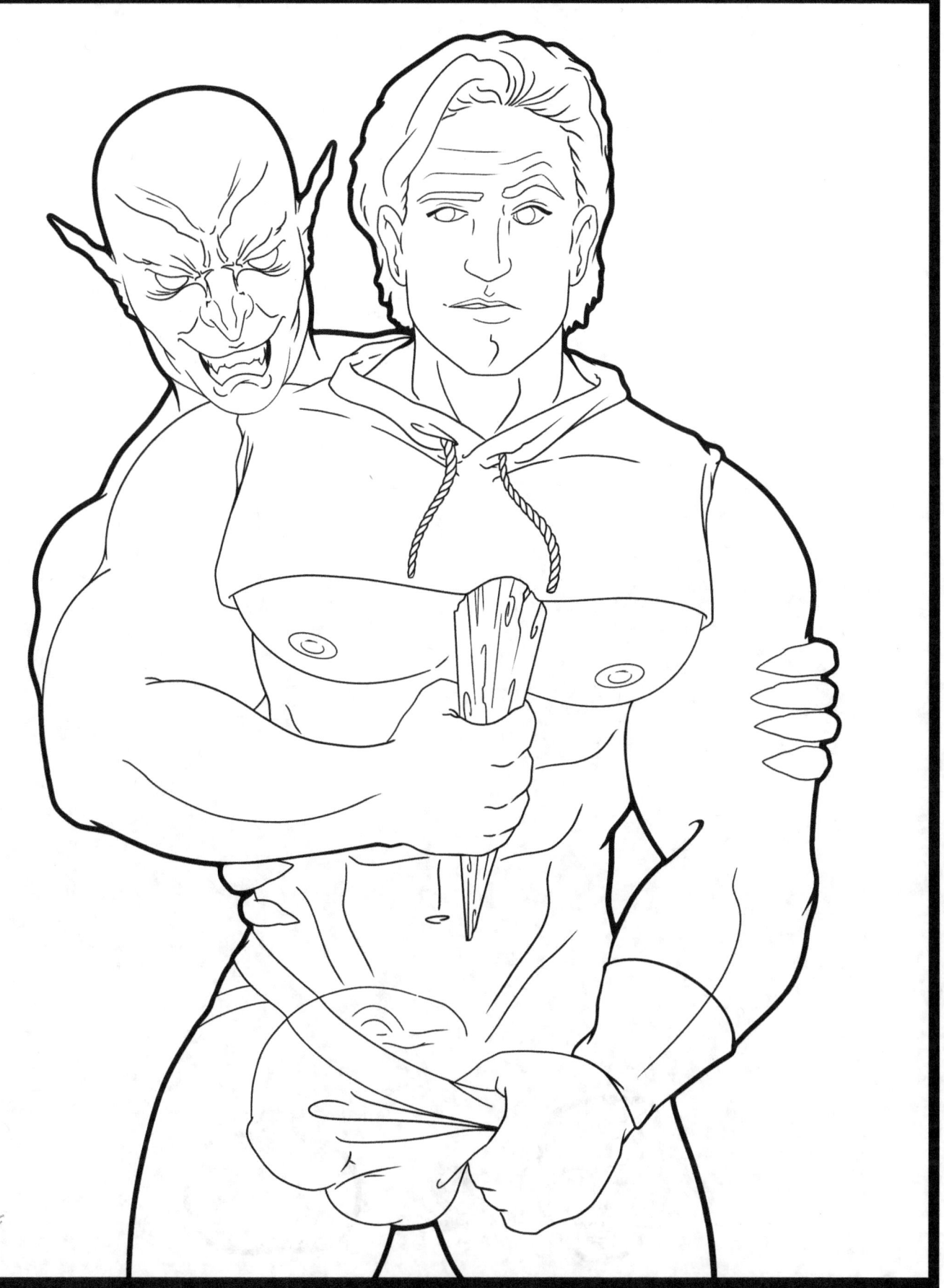

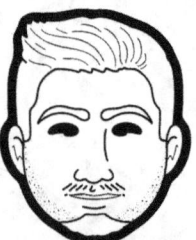 2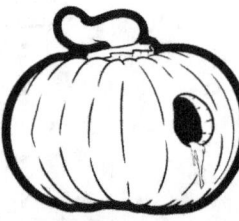

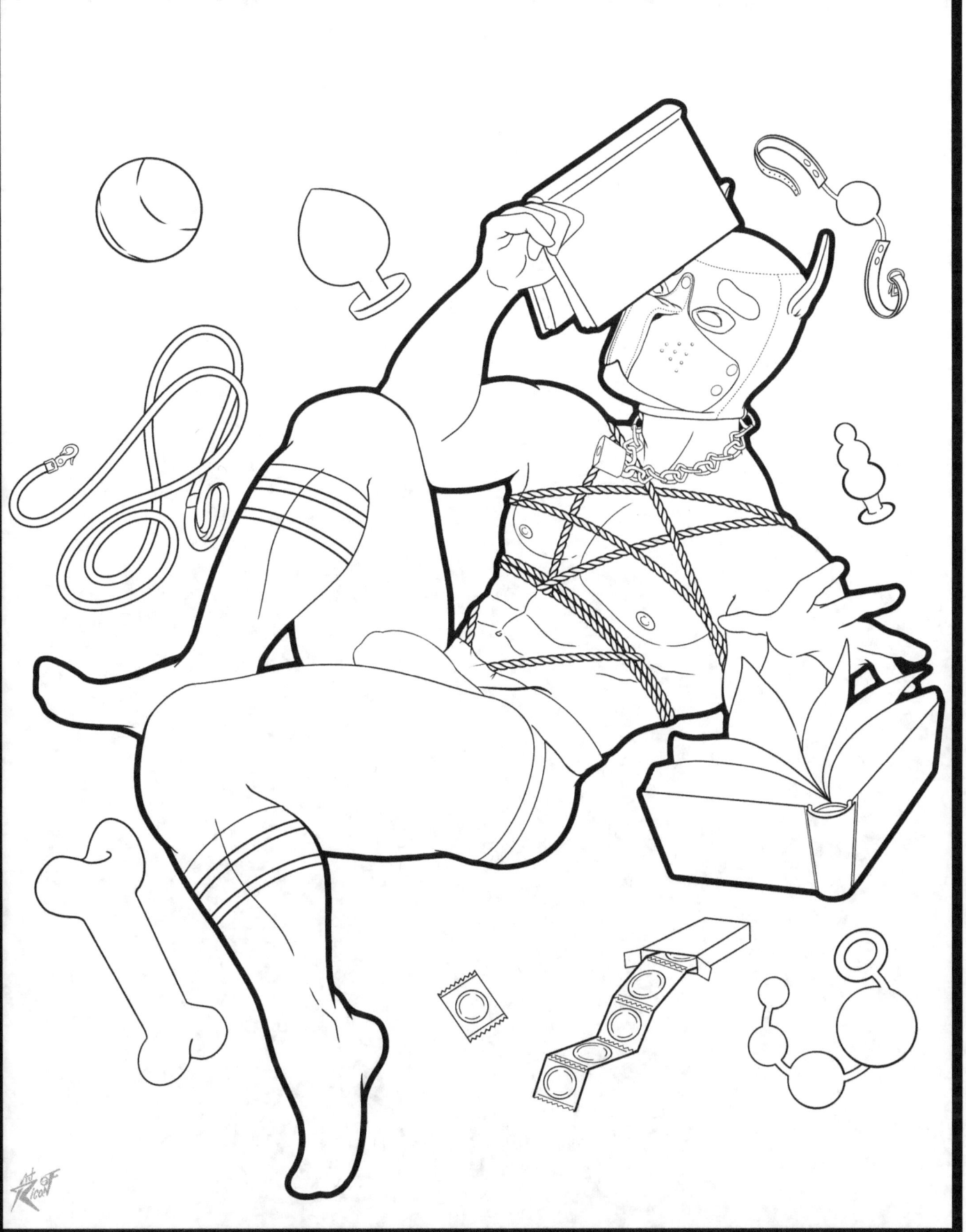

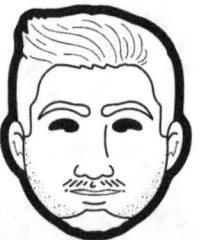 3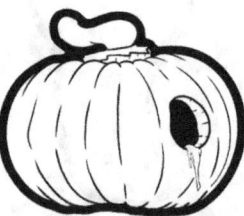

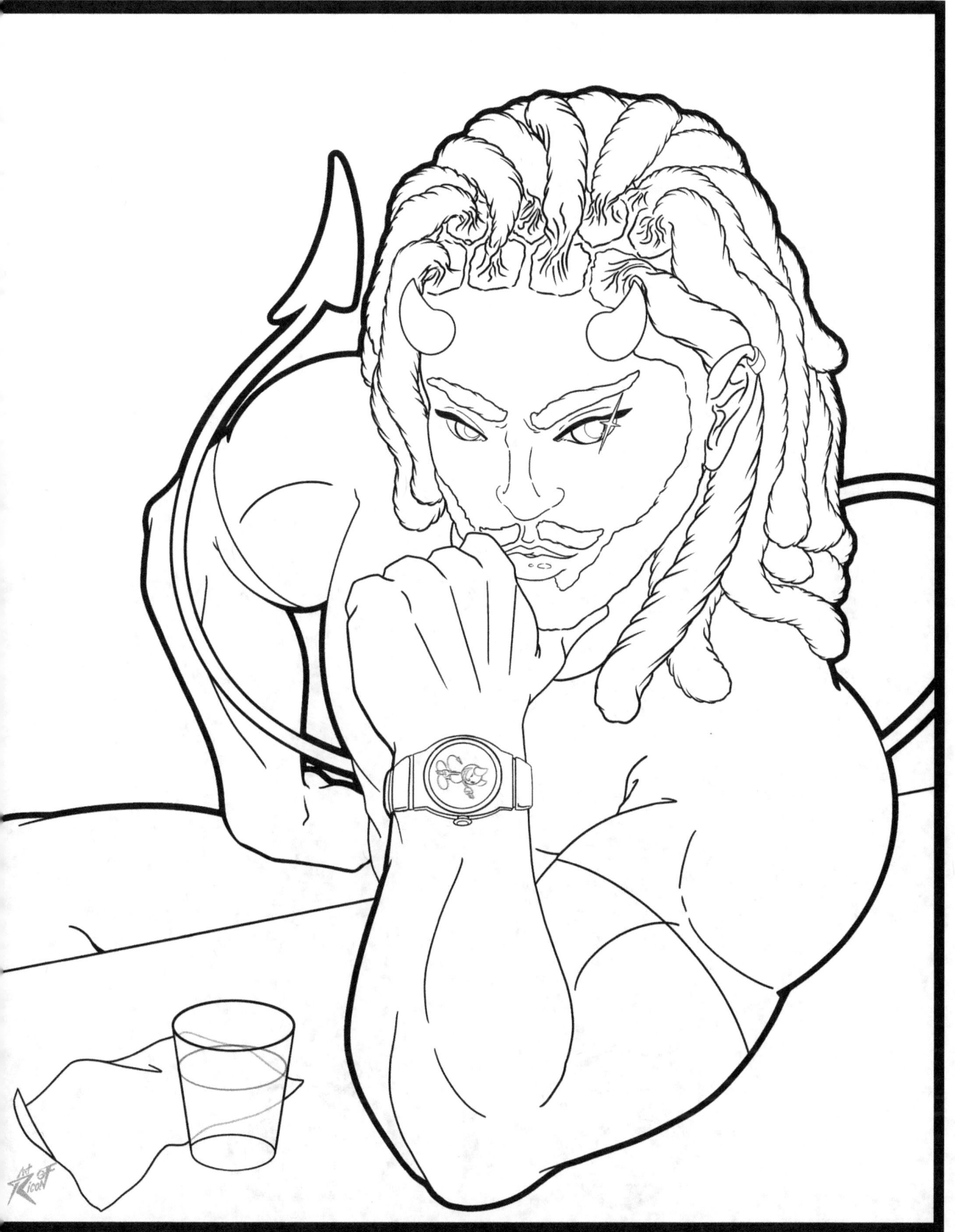

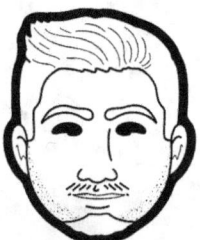 **4**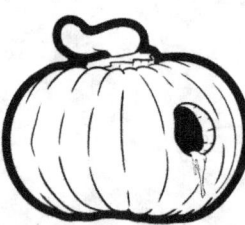

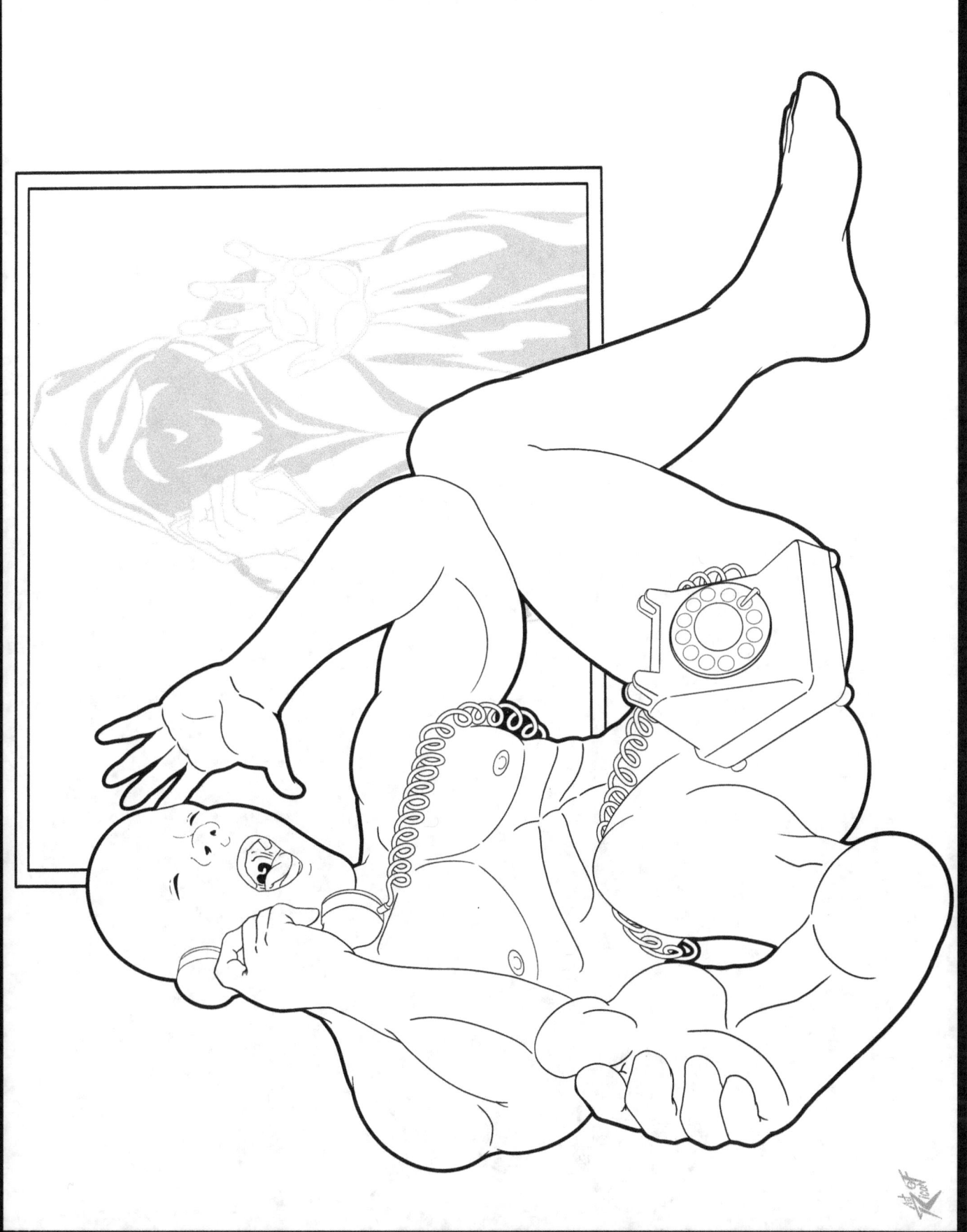

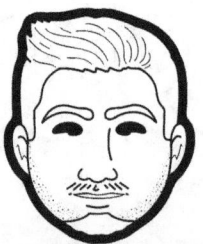 5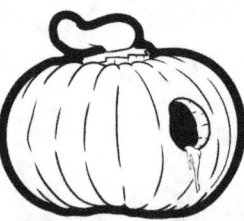

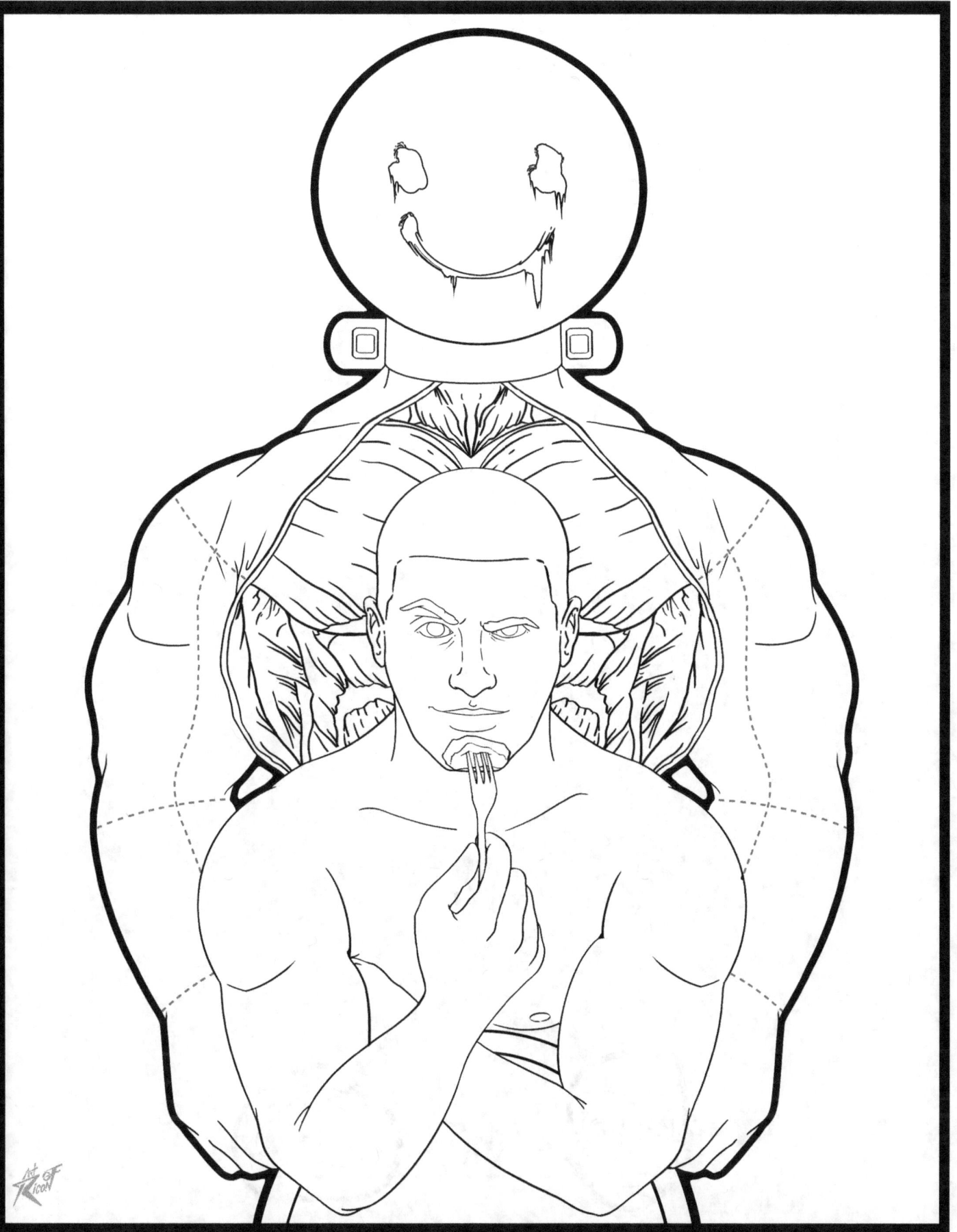

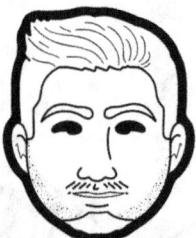 **6**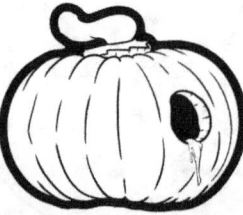

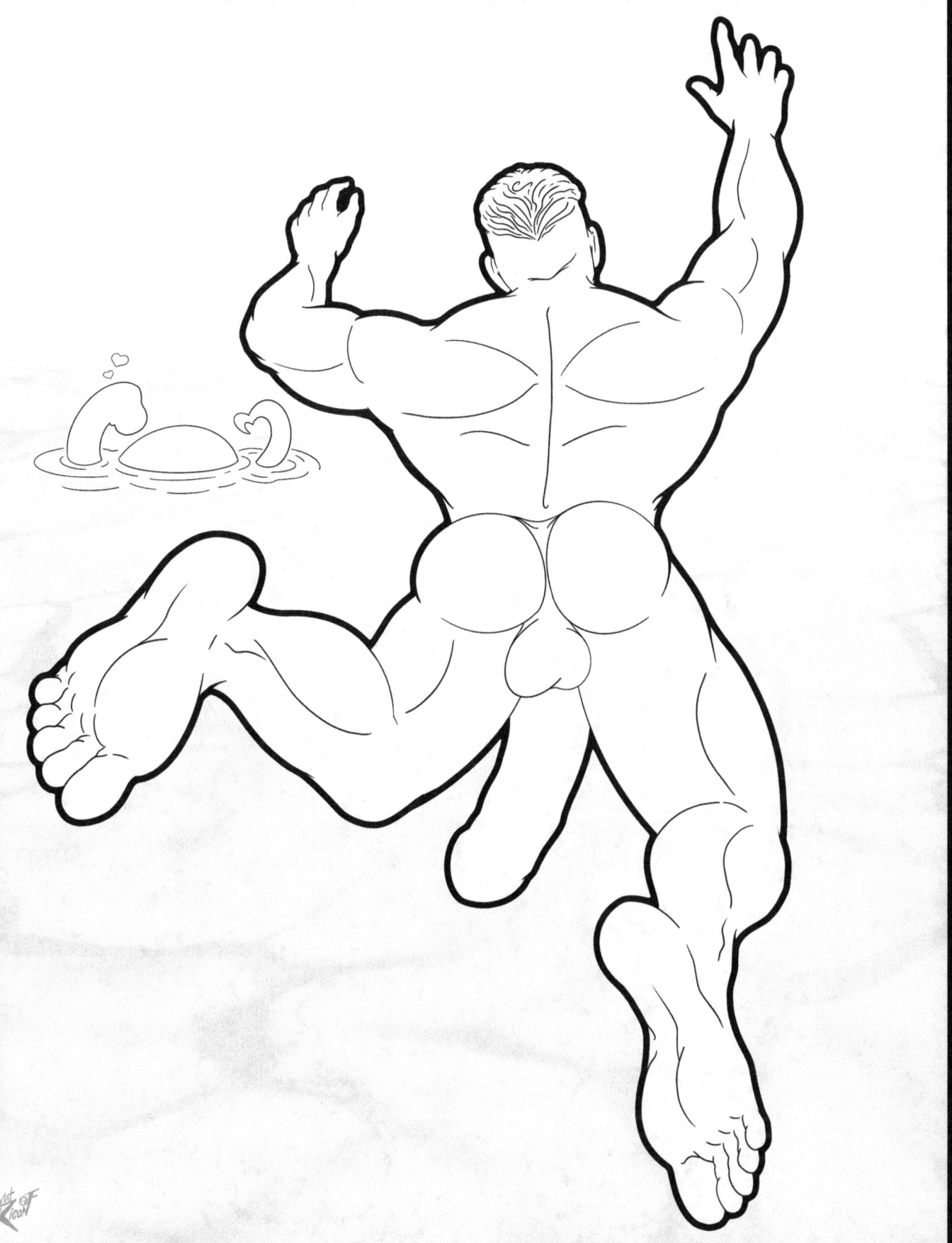

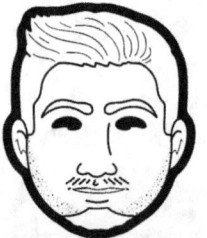 **7**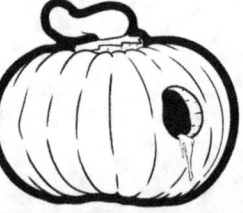

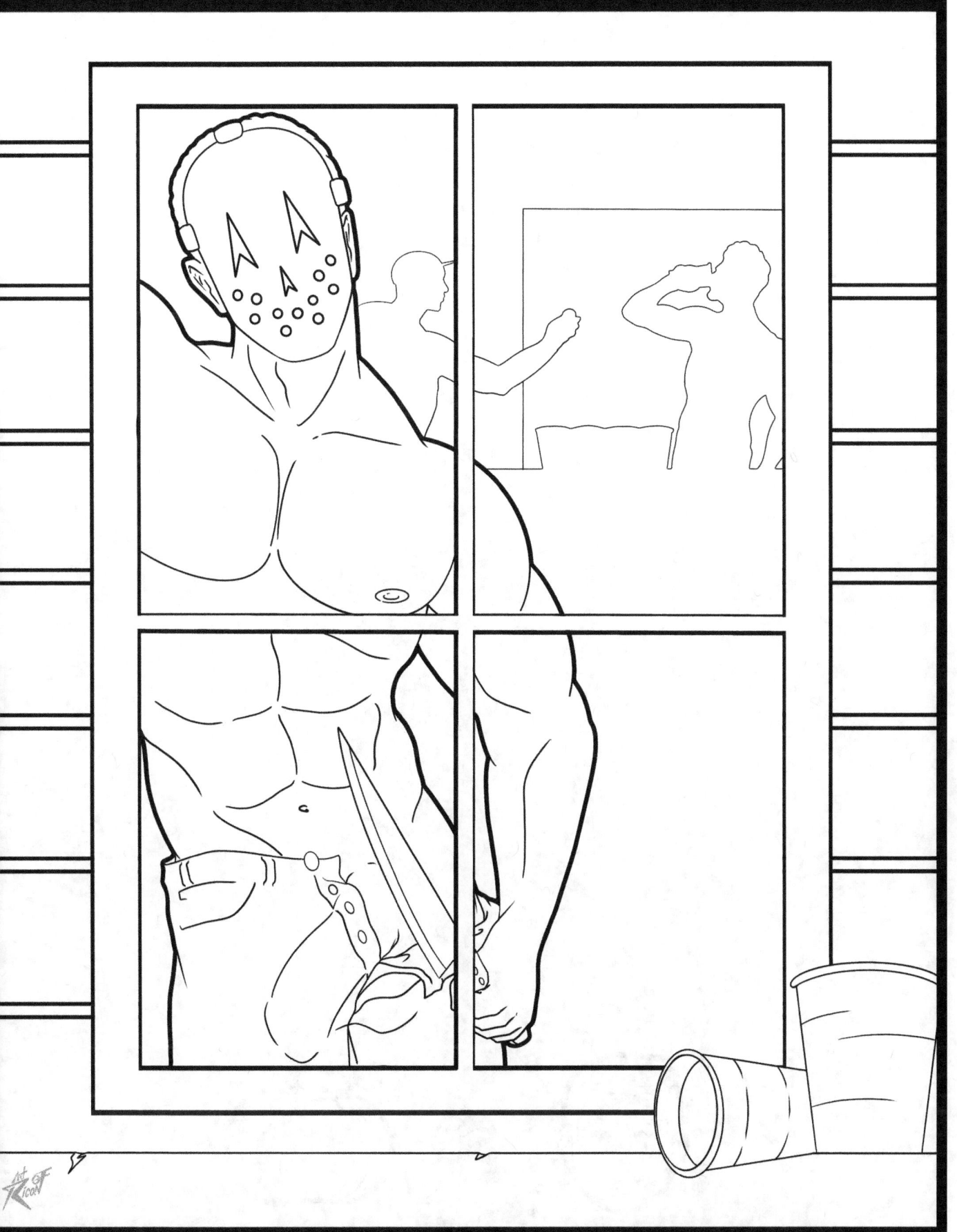

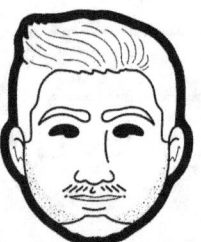 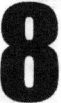 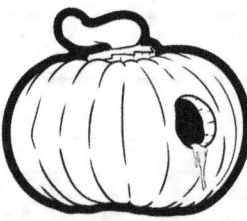

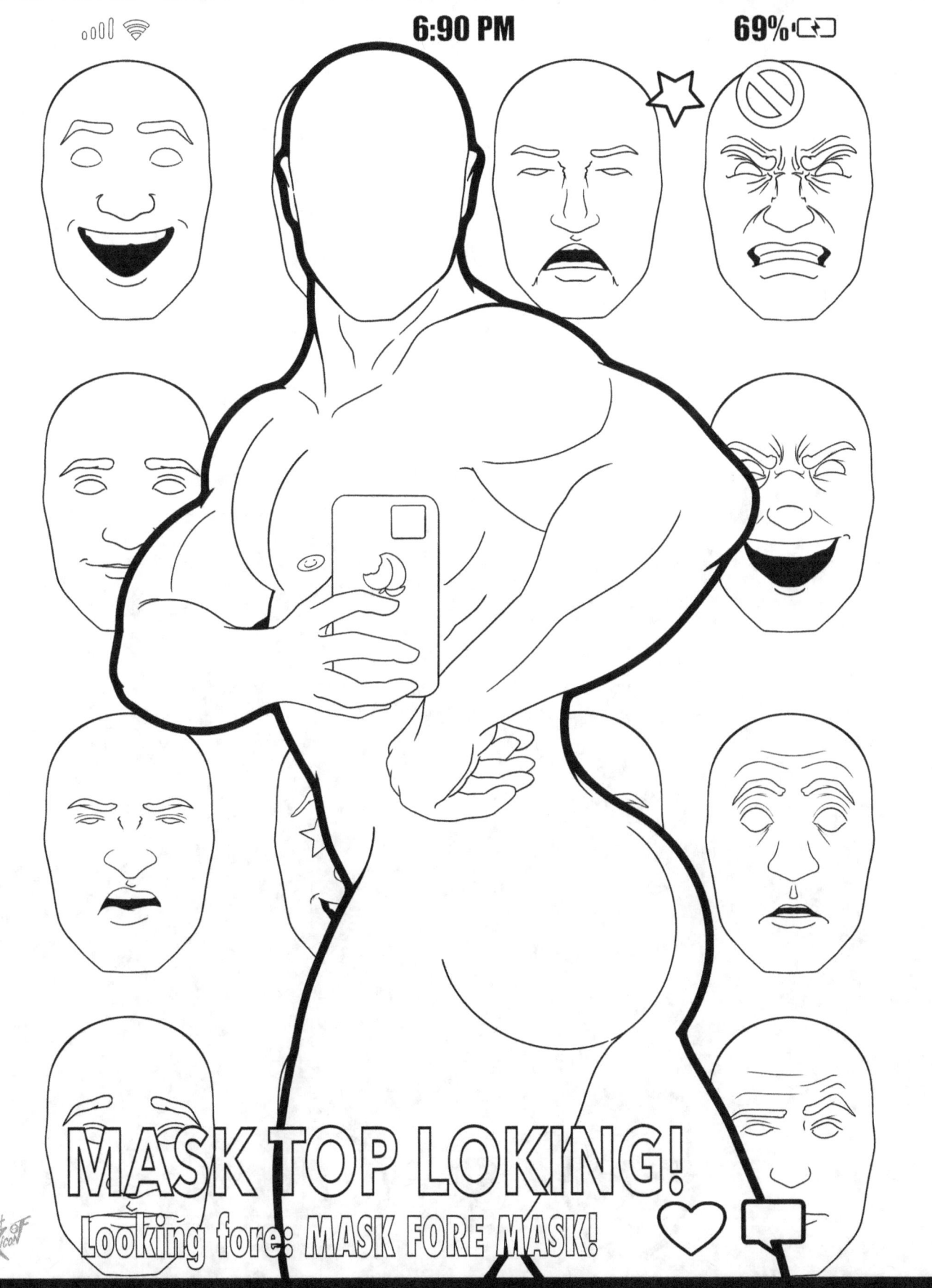

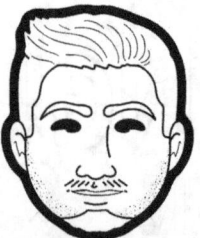 9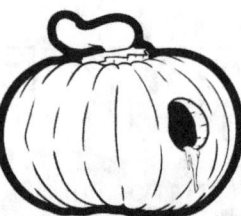

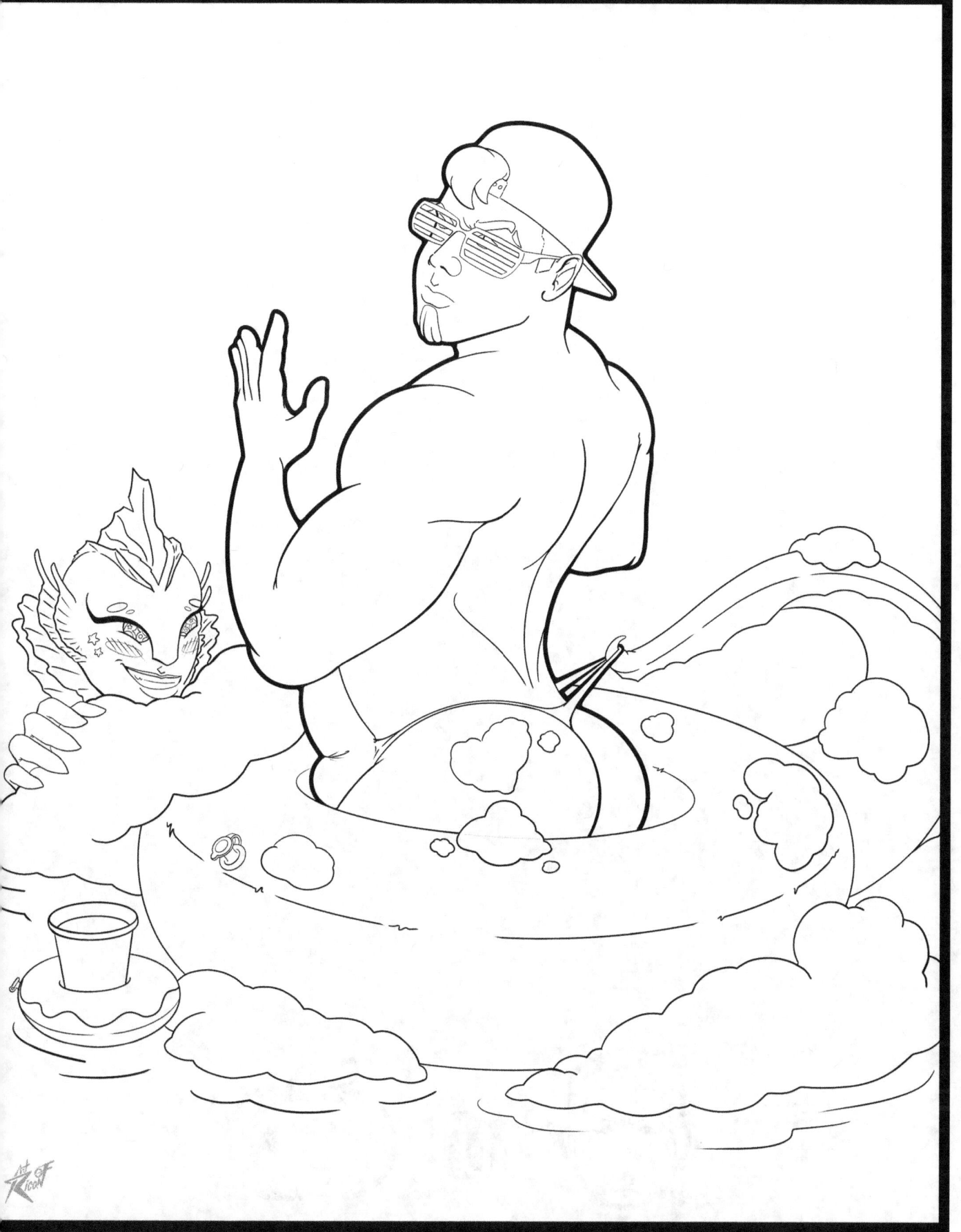

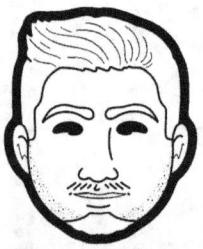 10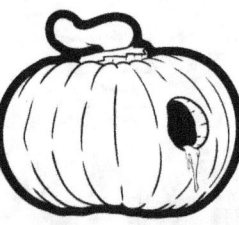

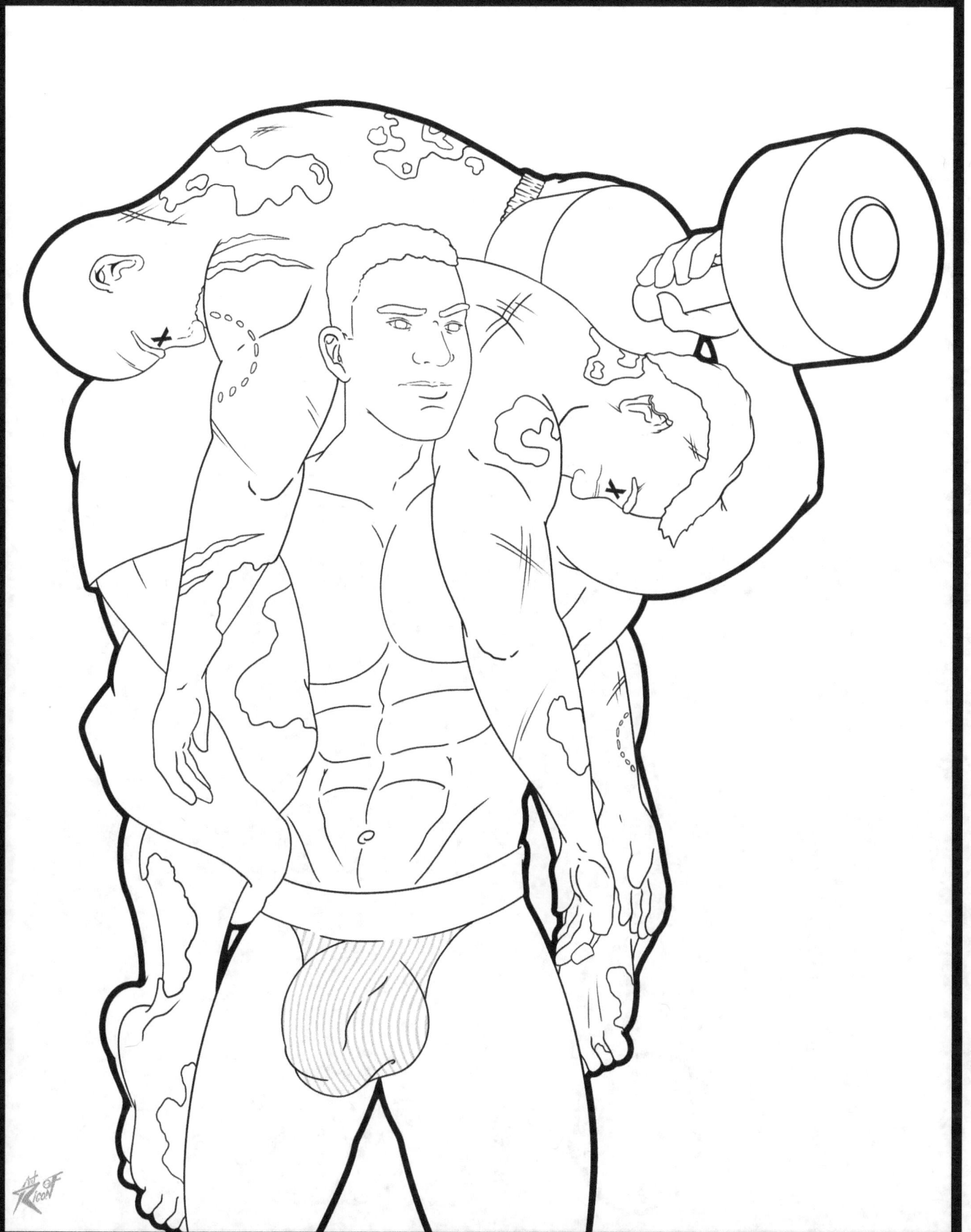

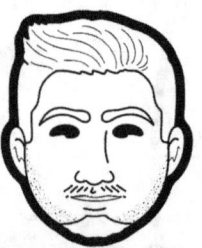 **11**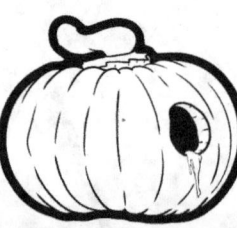

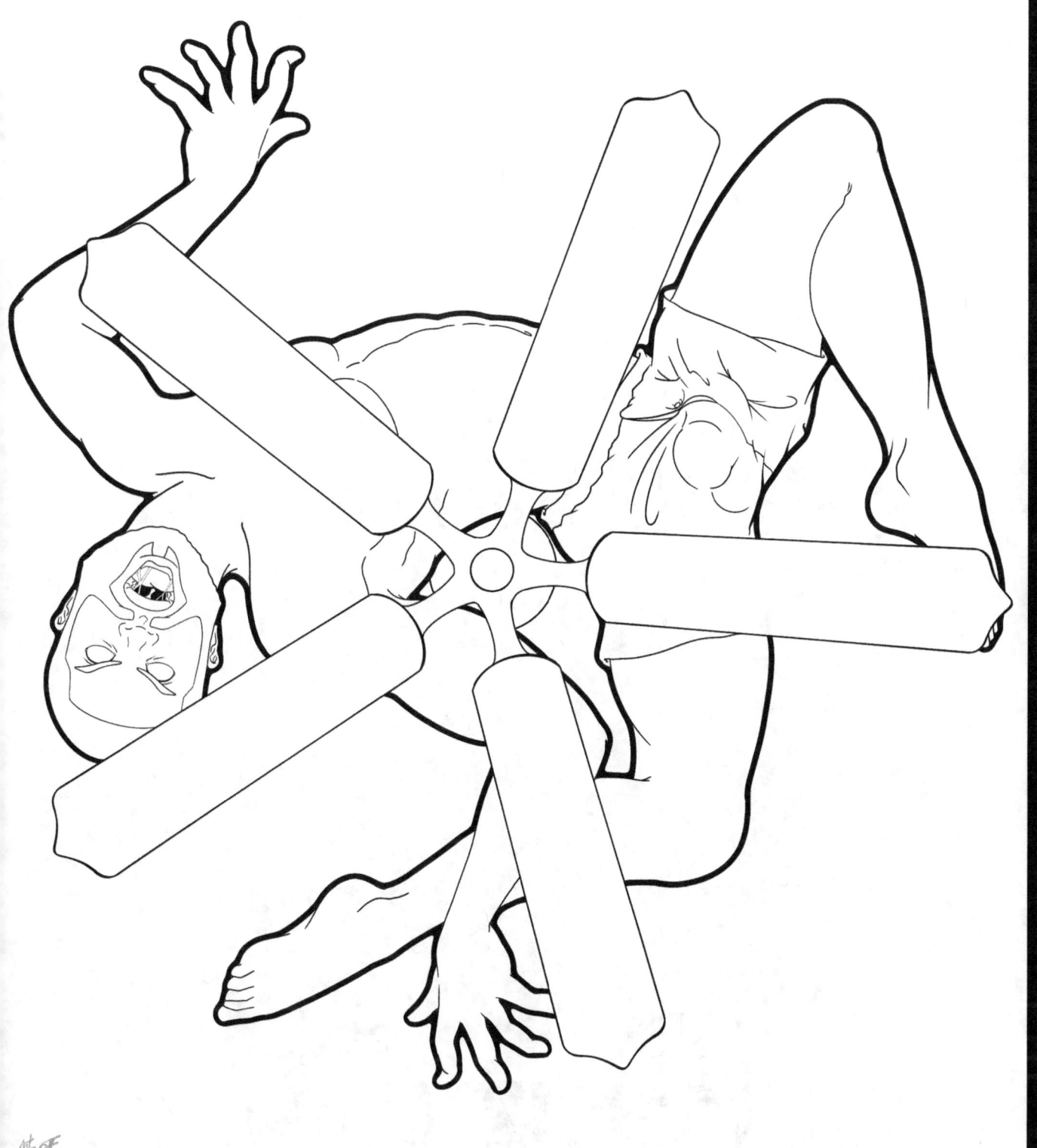

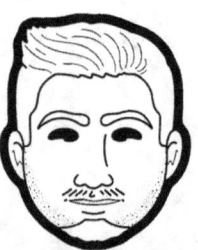 **12**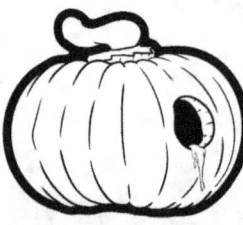

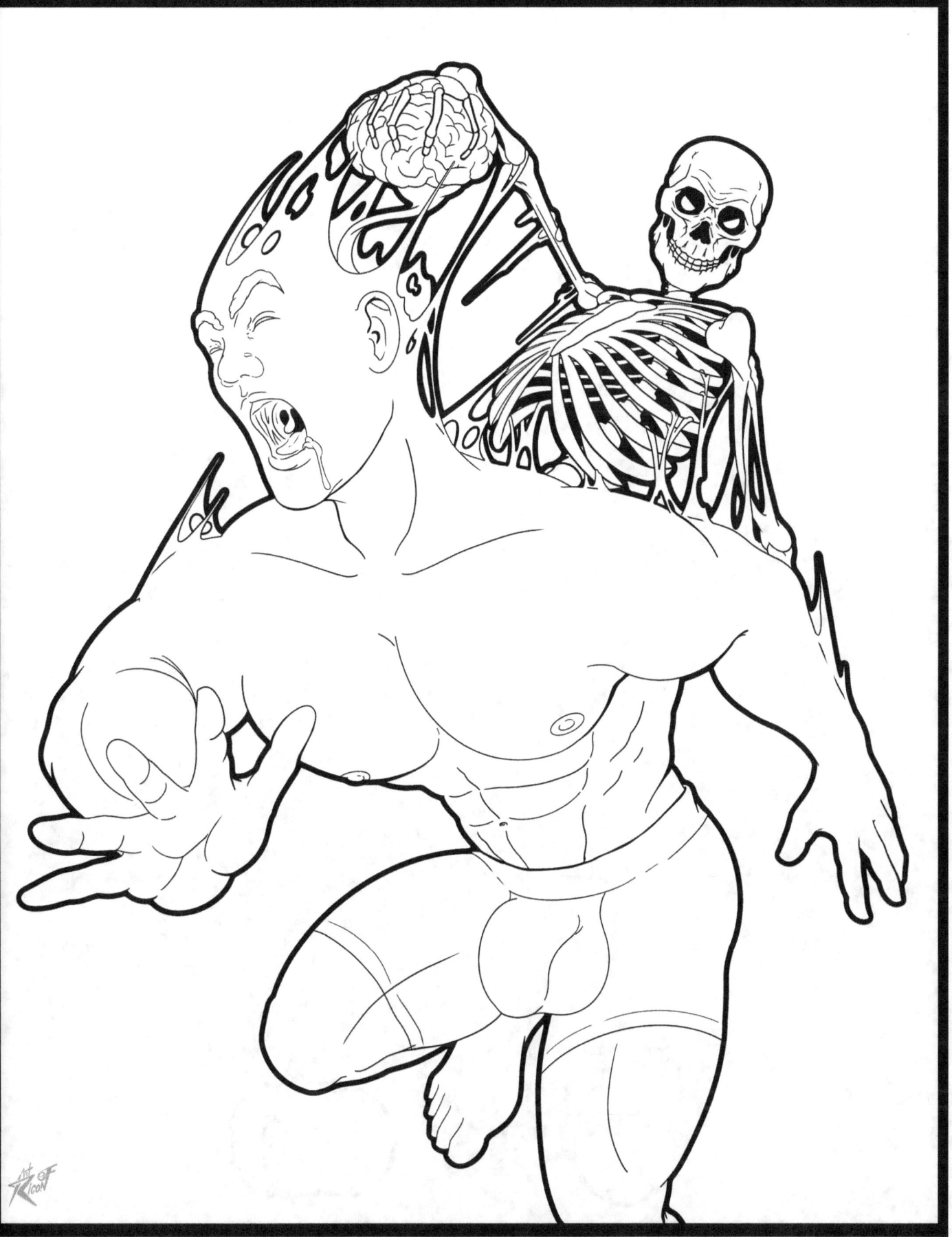

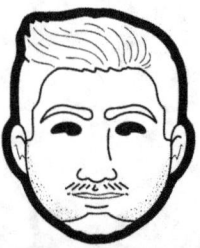 **13**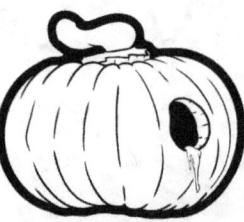

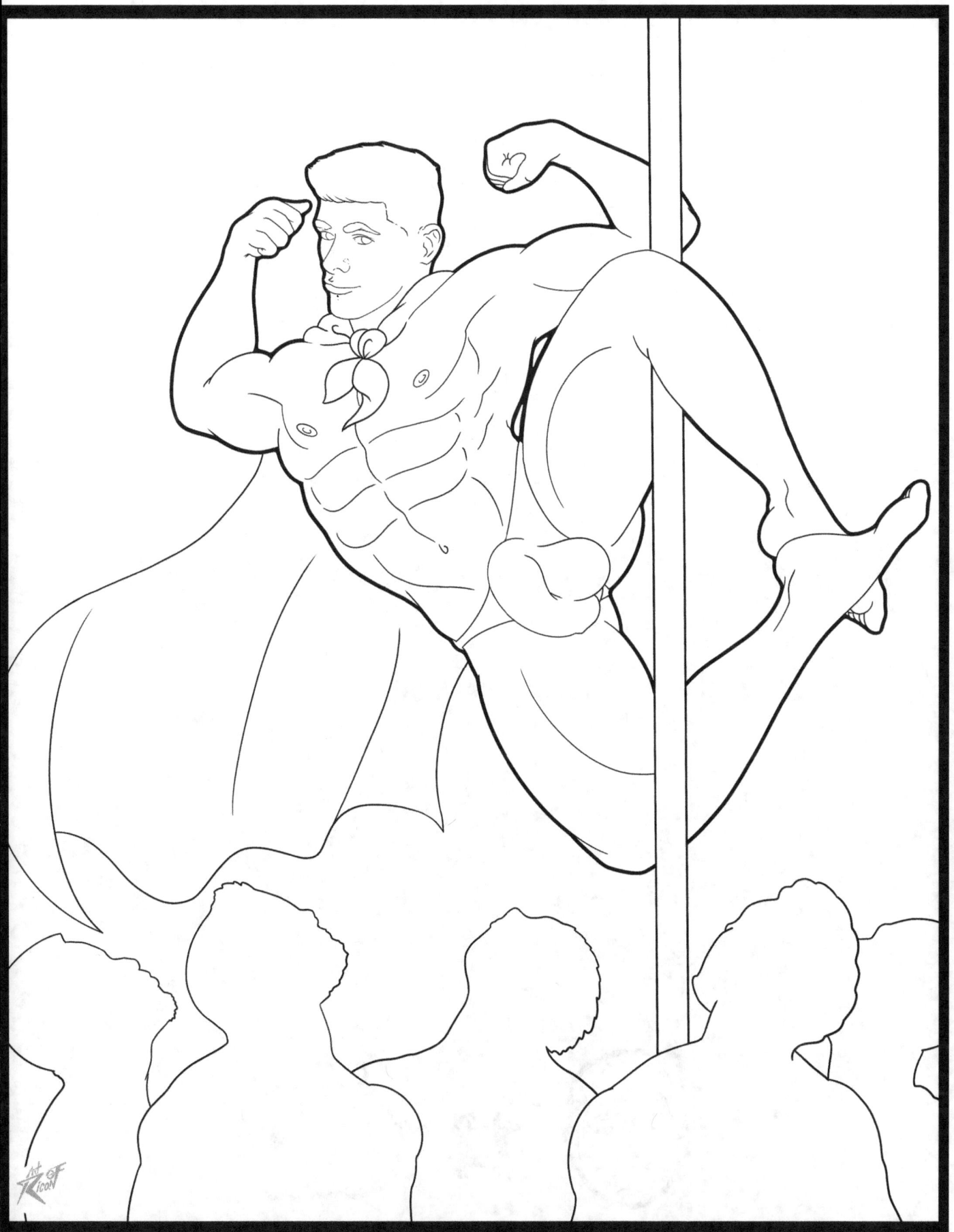

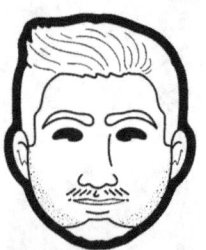 **14**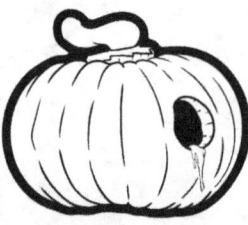

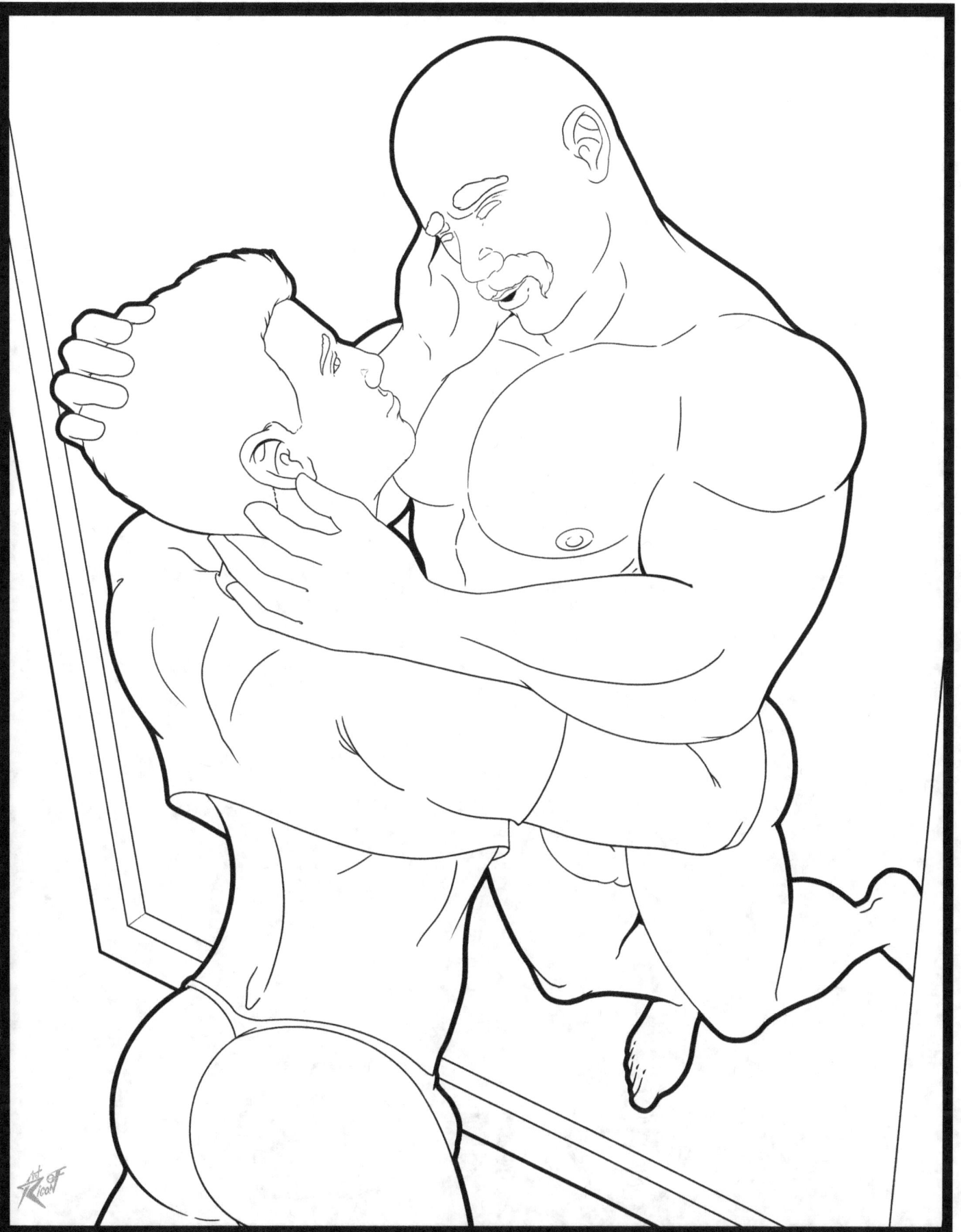

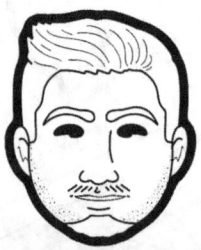 **15**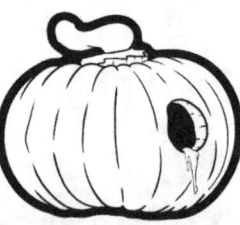

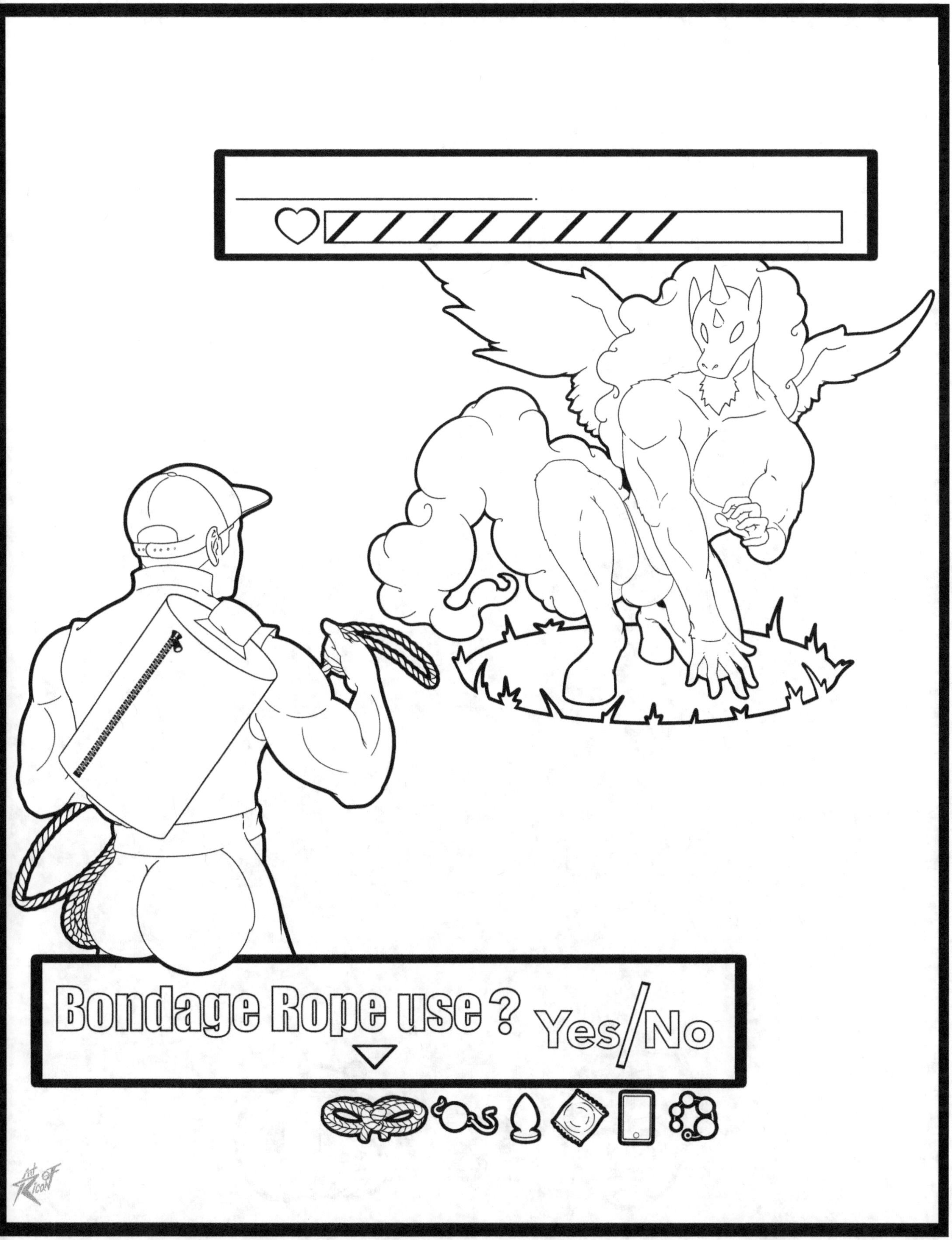

Bondage Rope use ? Yes/No

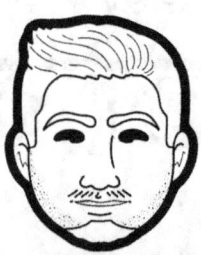 16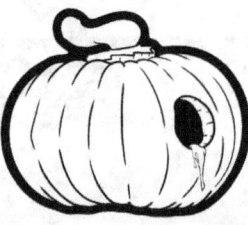

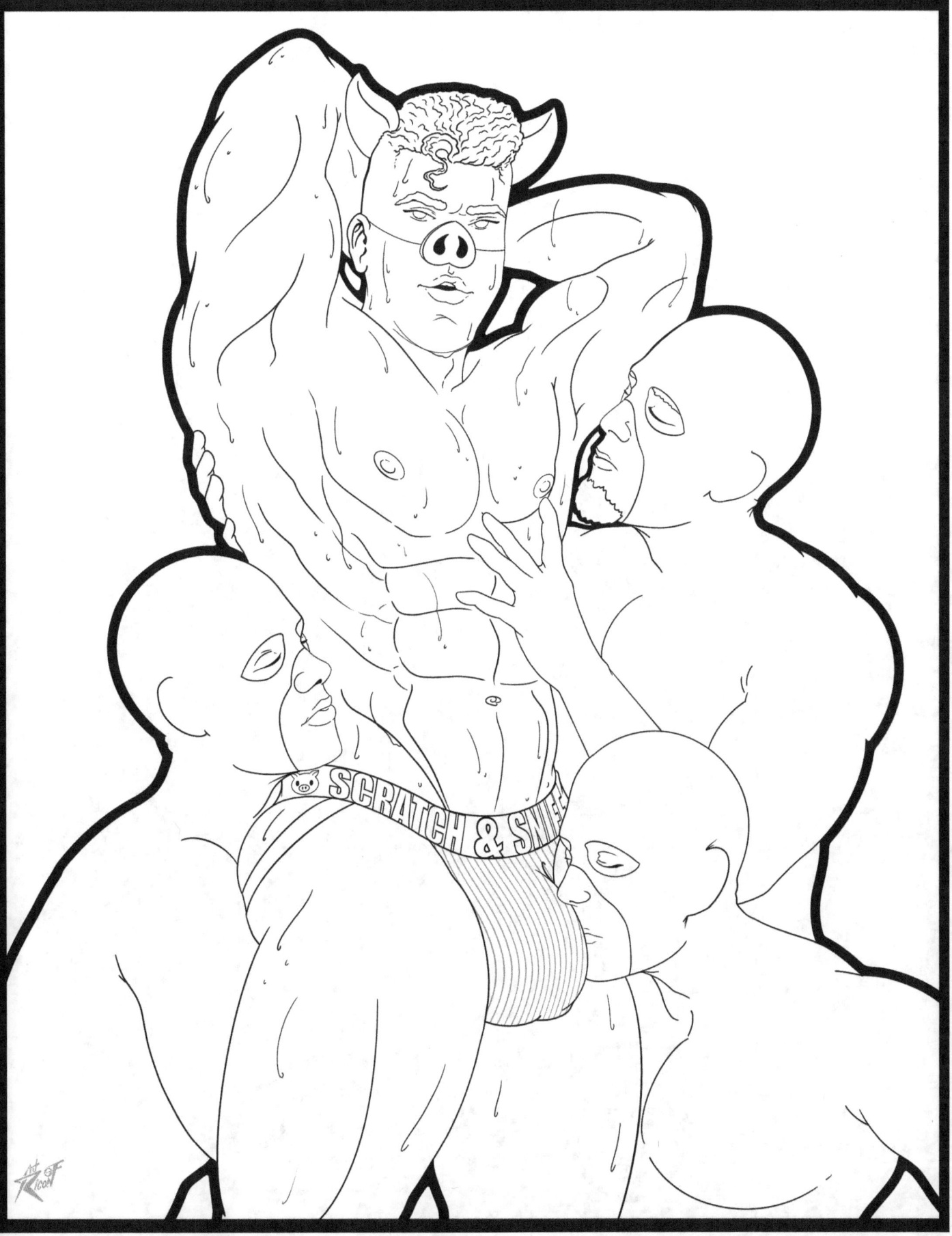

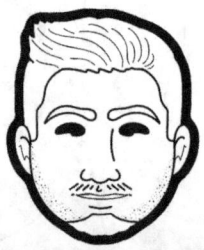 **17**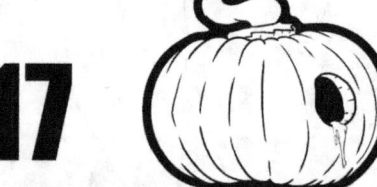

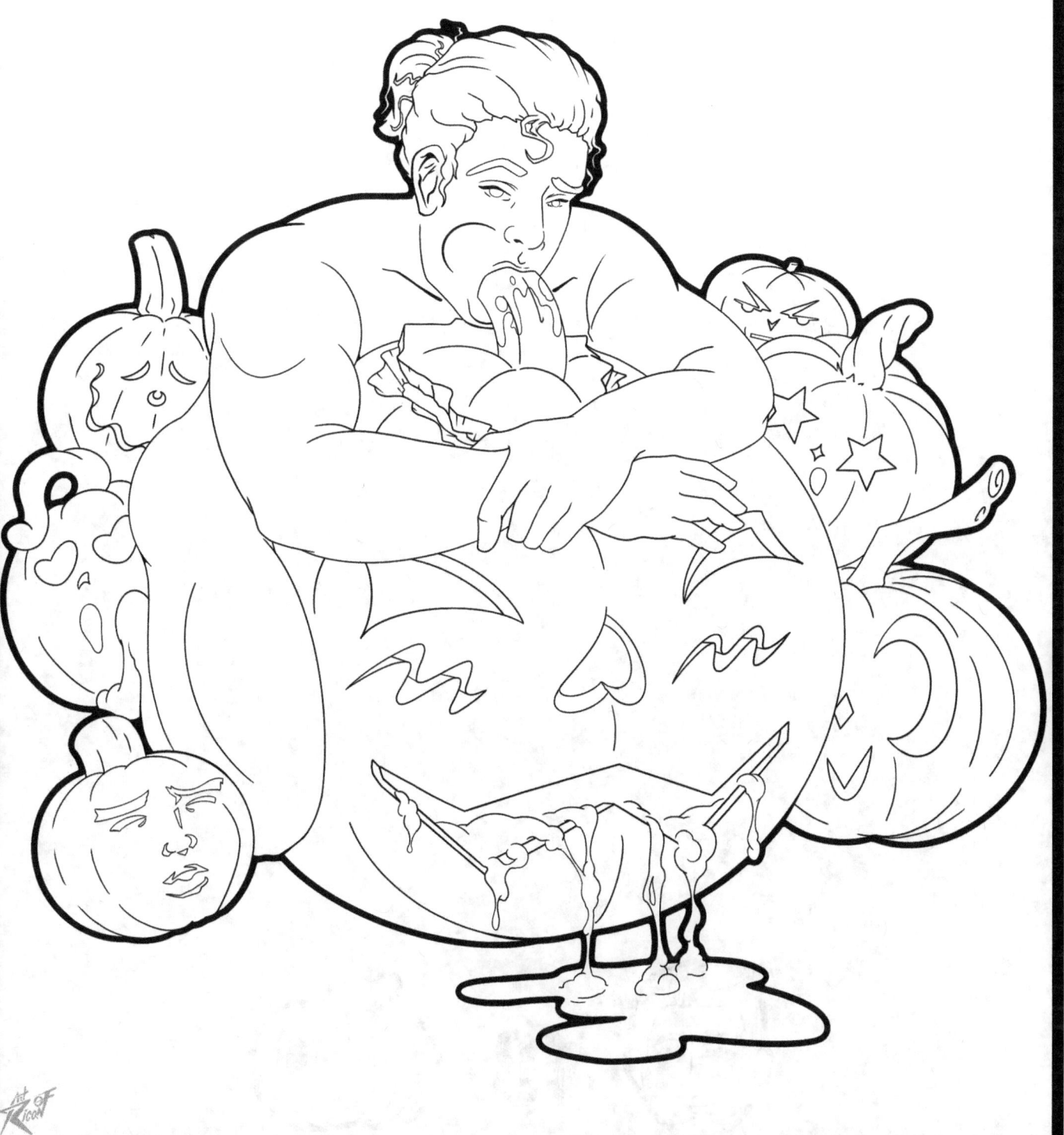

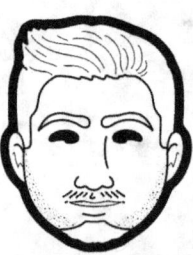 **18**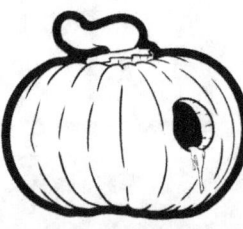

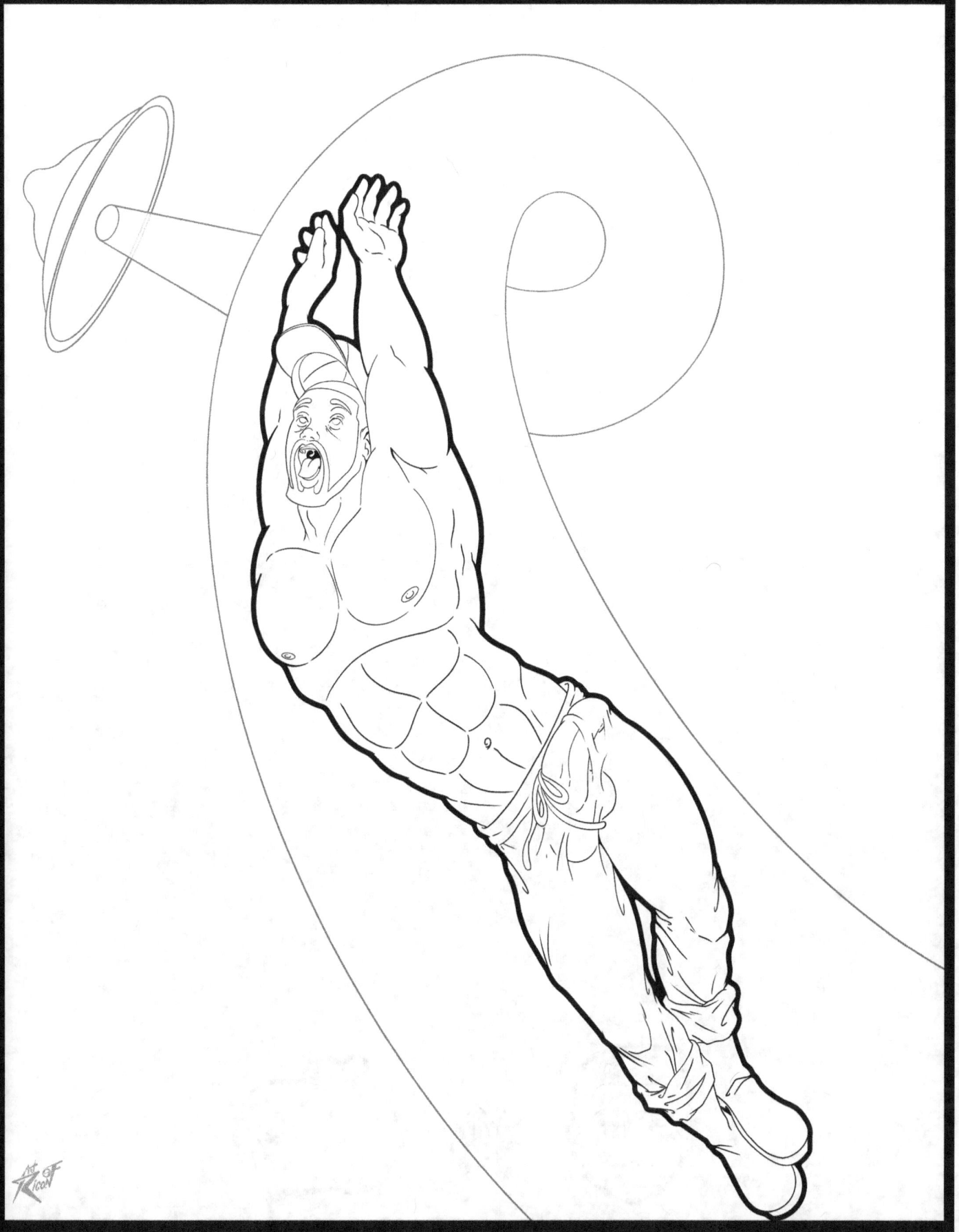

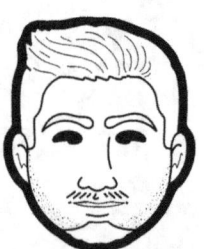 **19**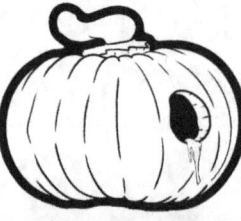

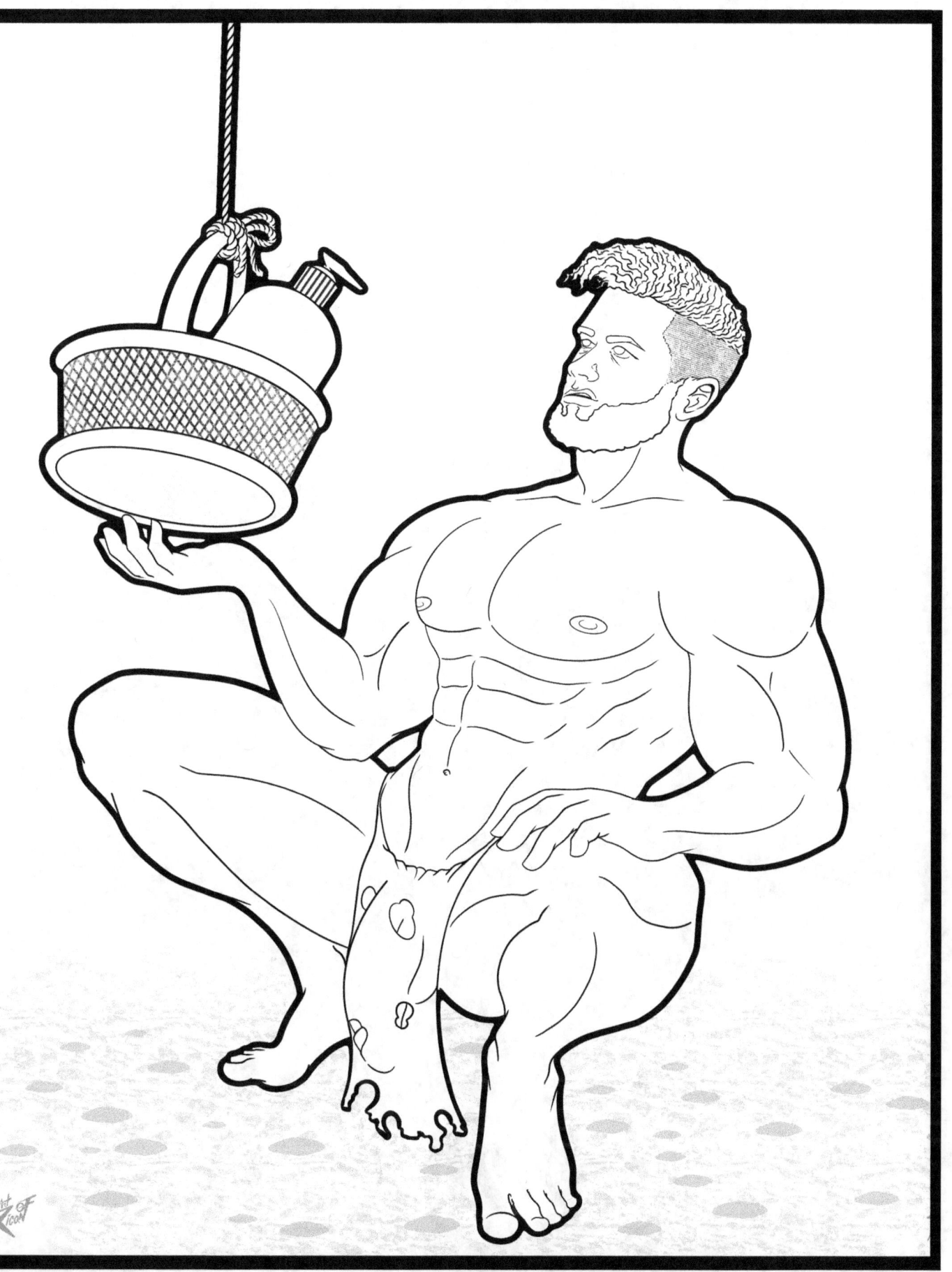

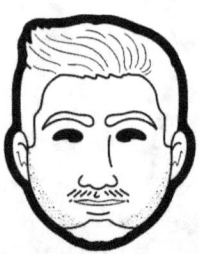 **20**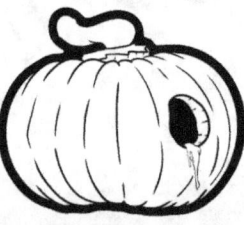

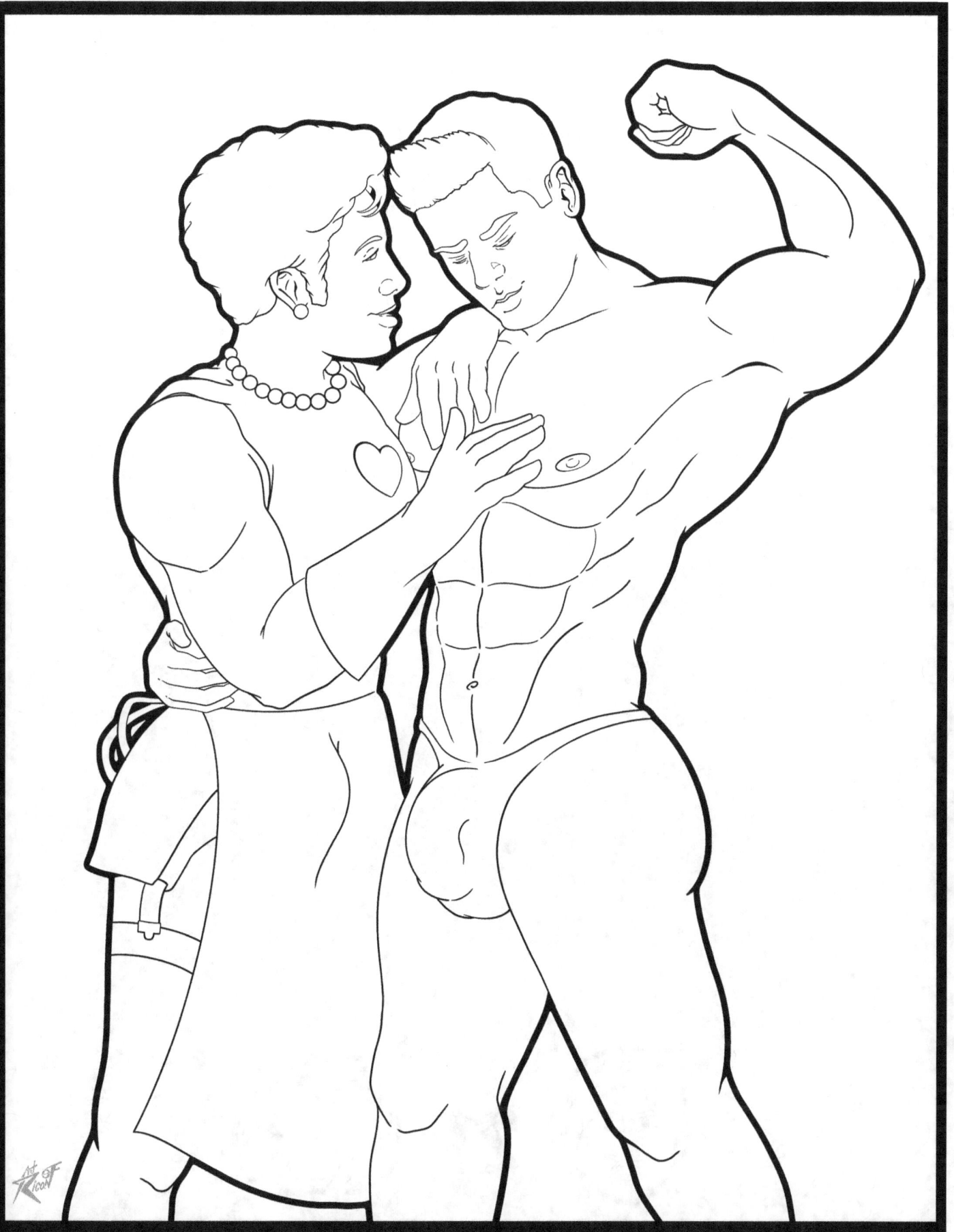

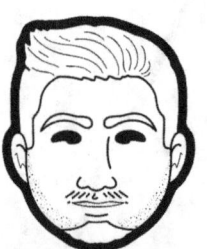 21

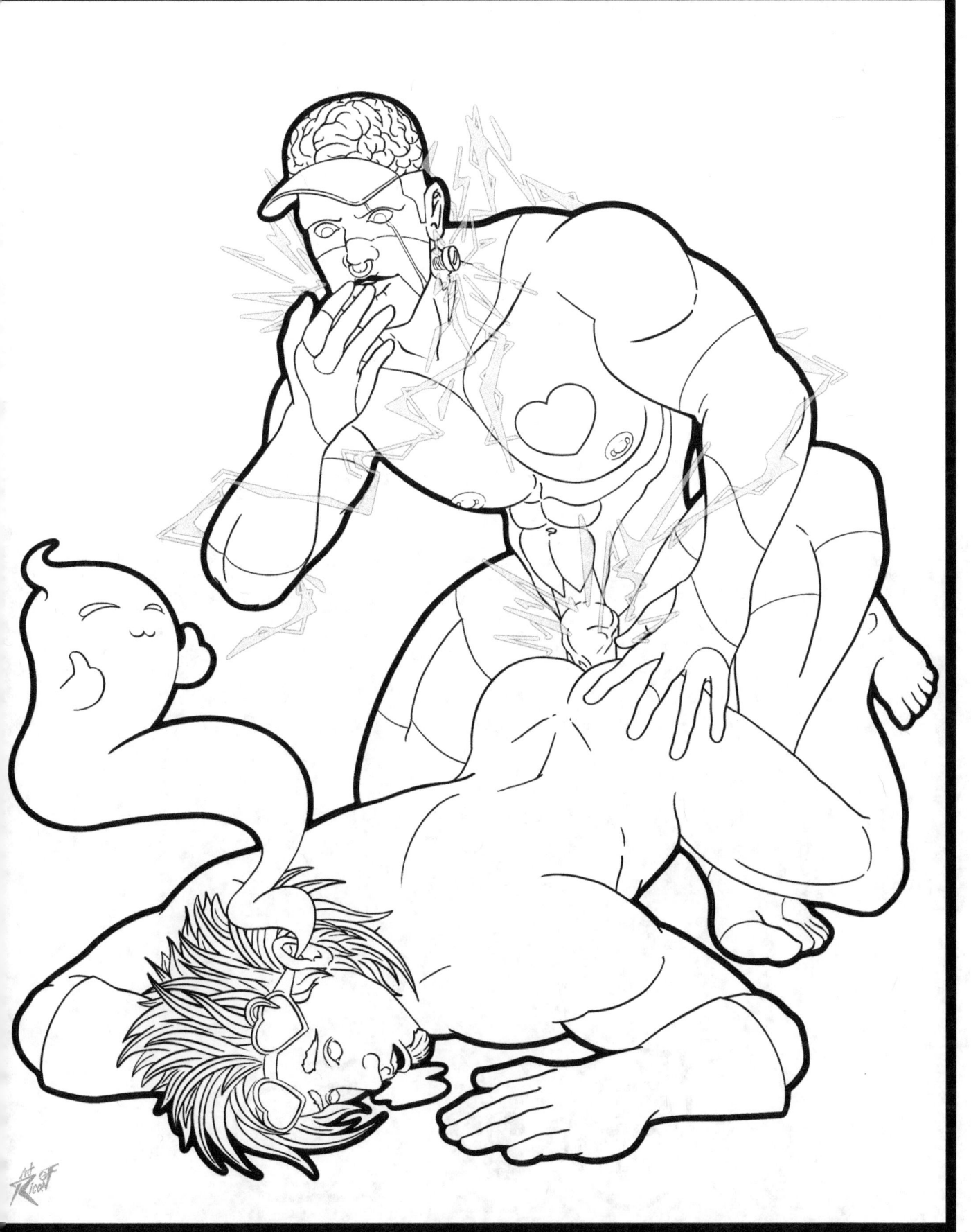

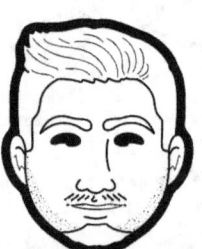 22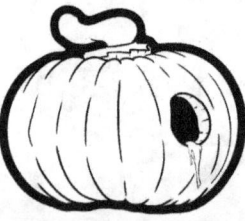

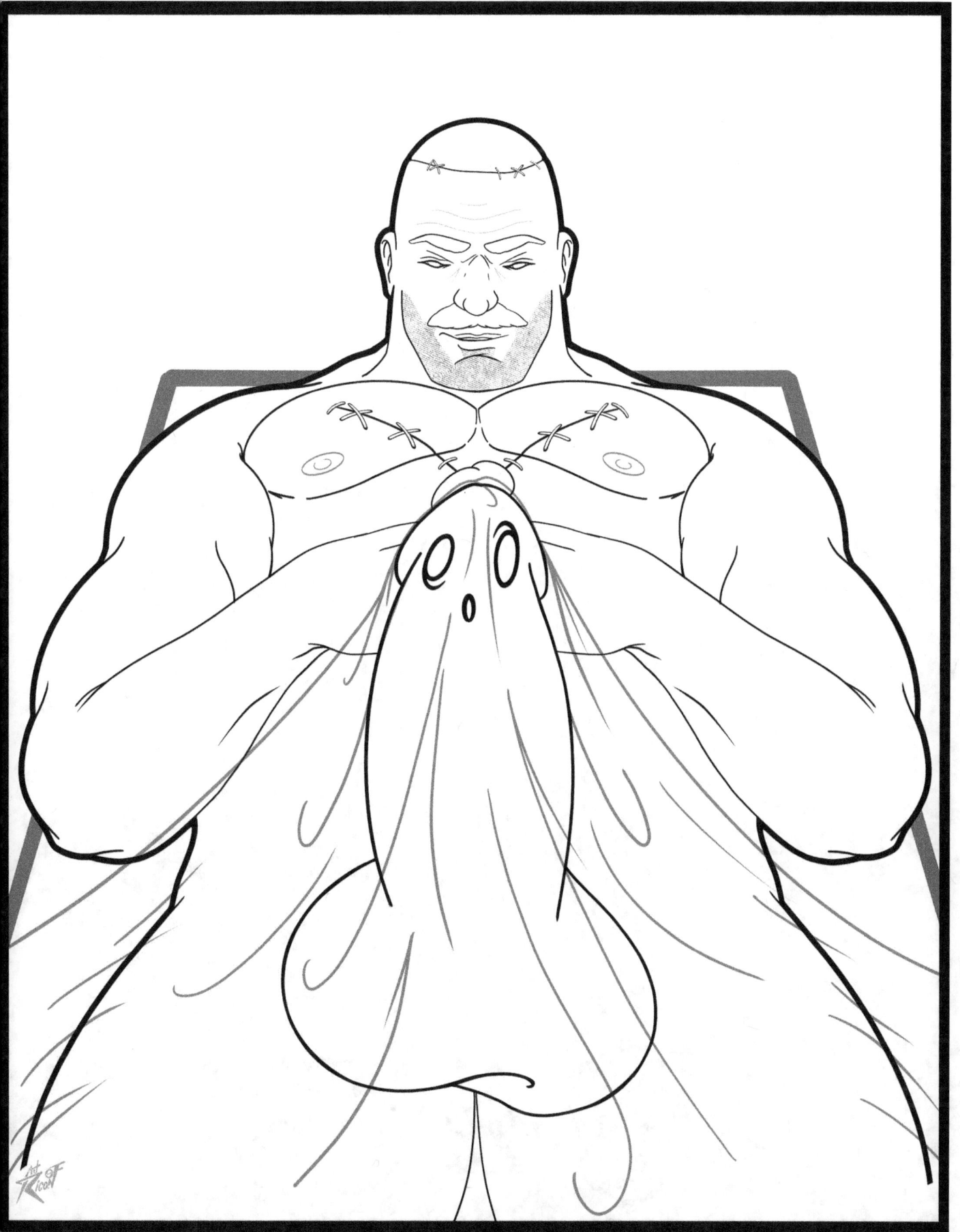

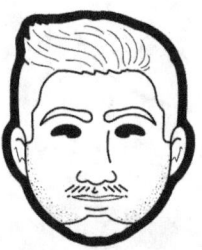 23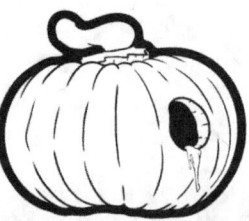

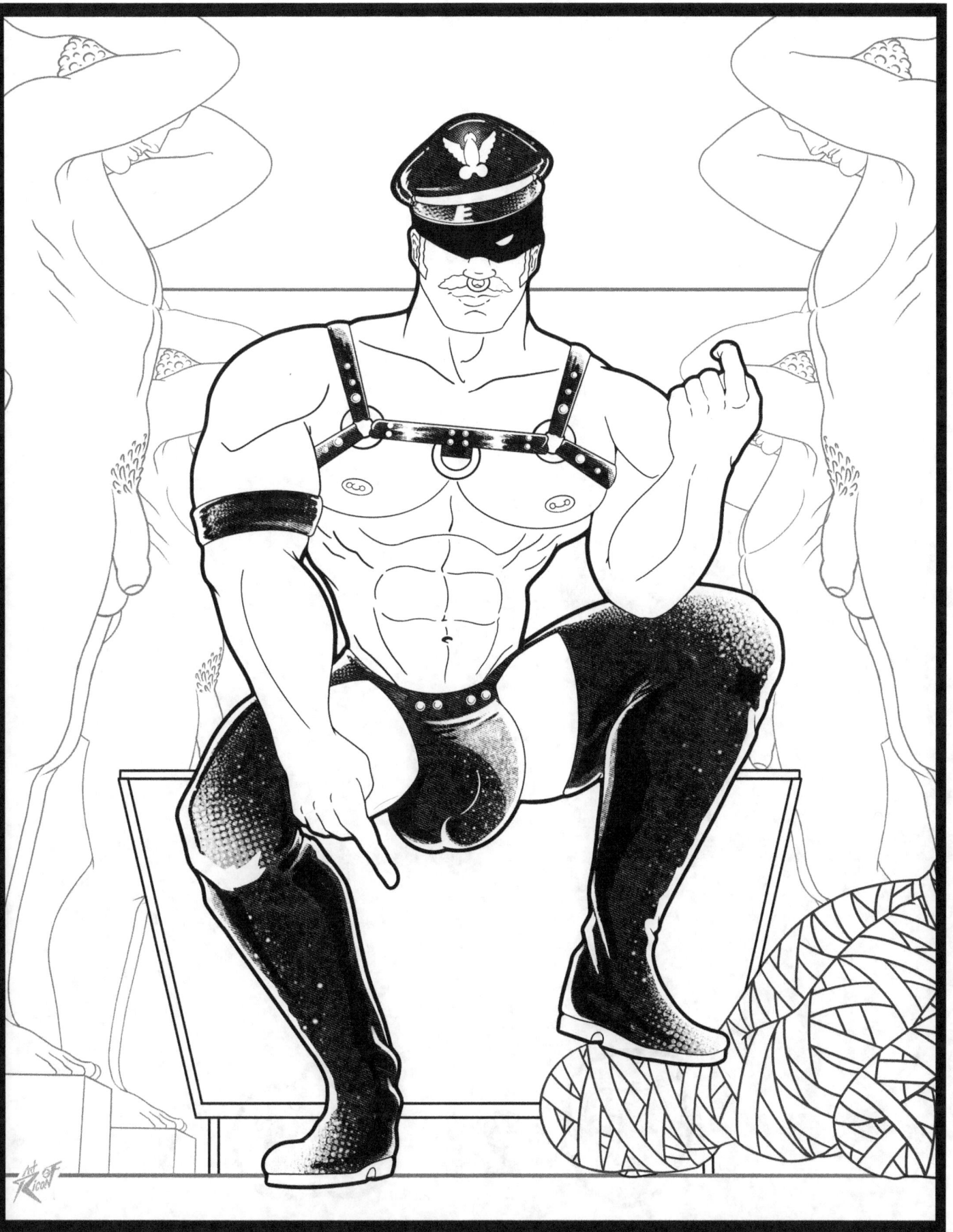

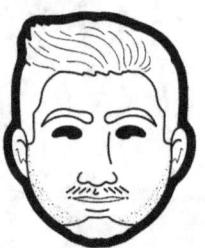 **24**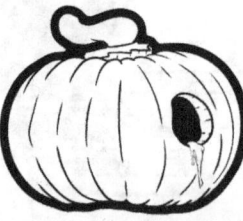

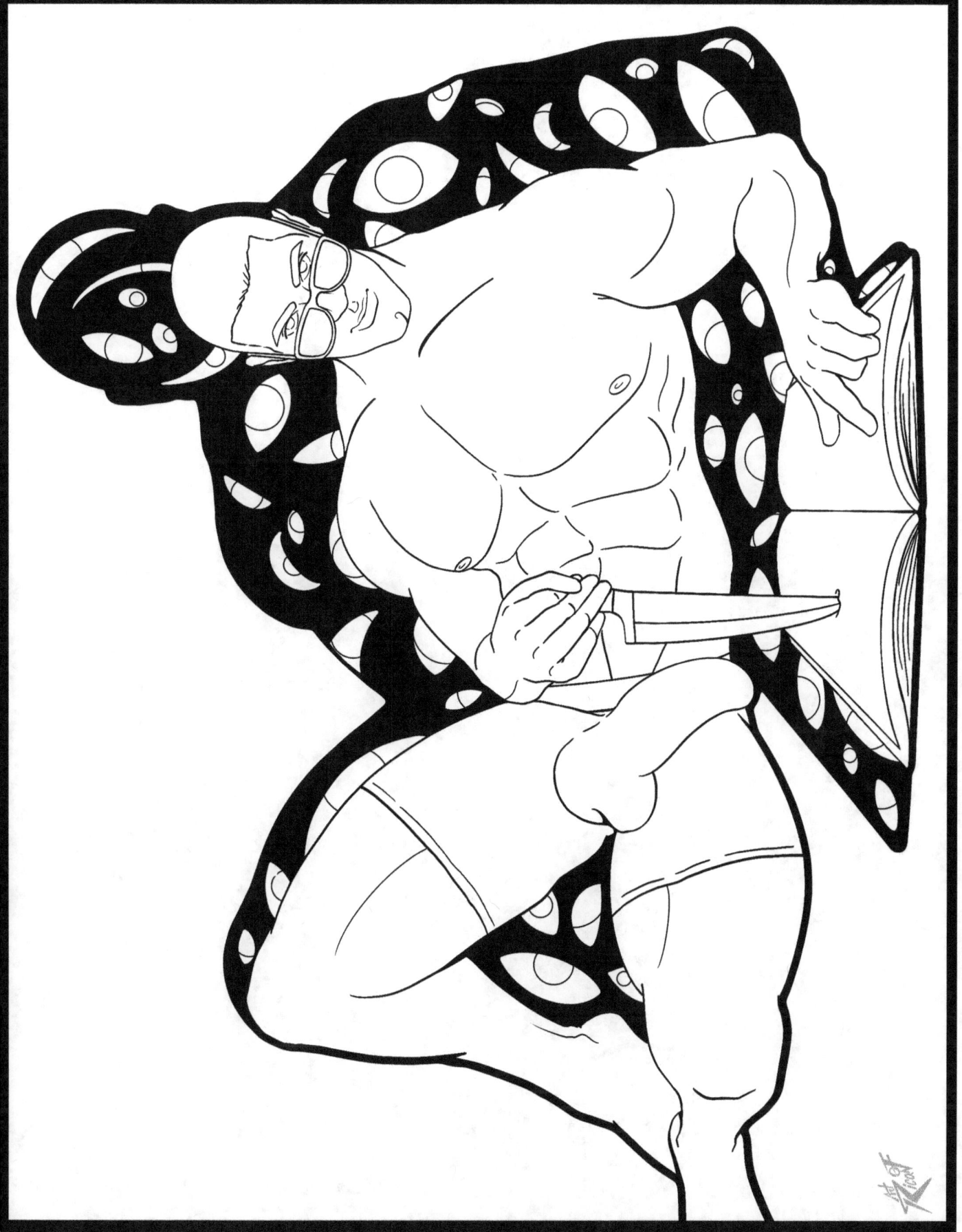

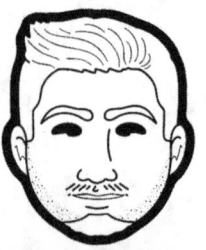 25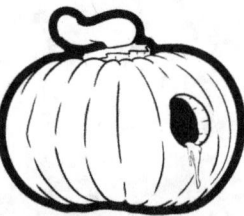

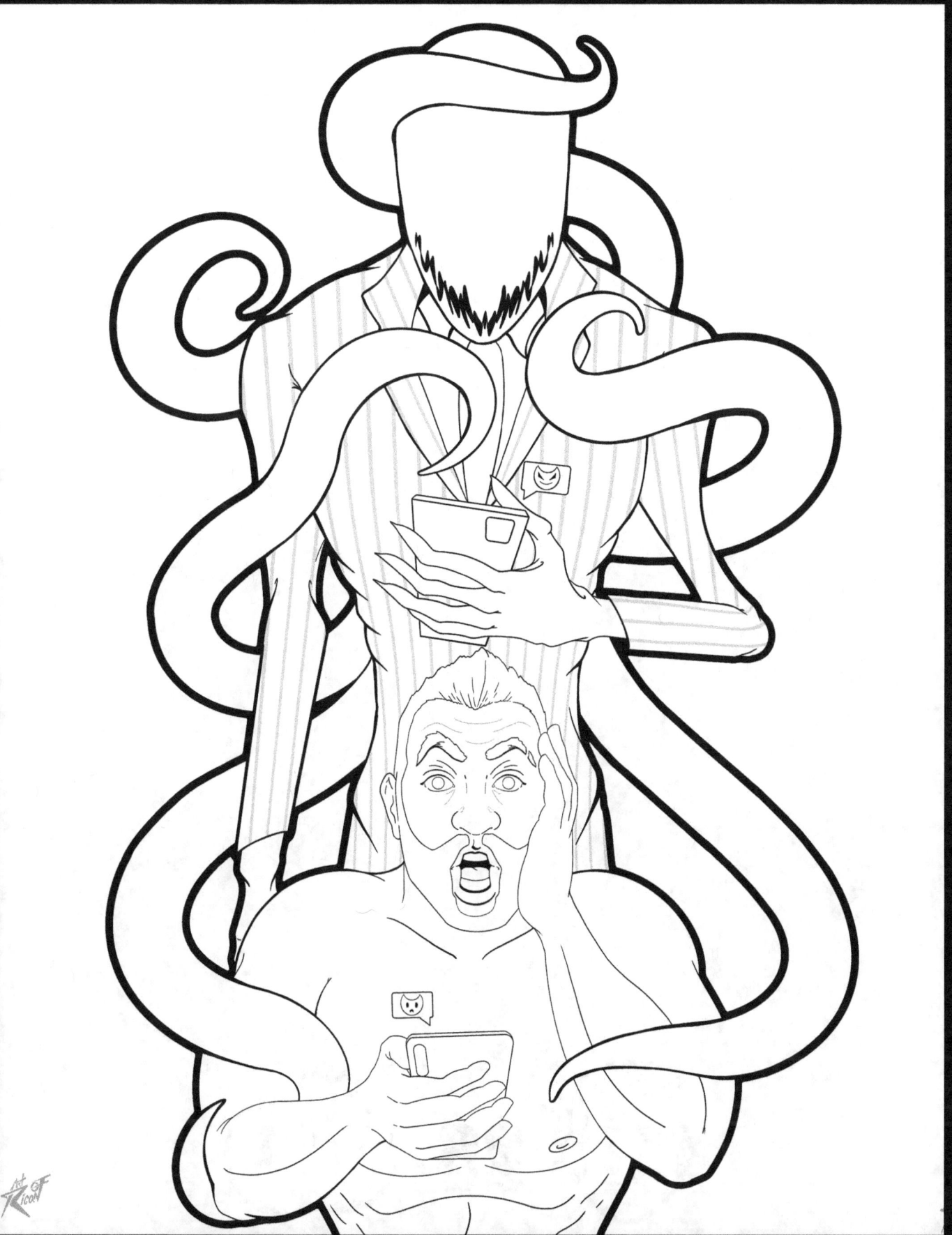

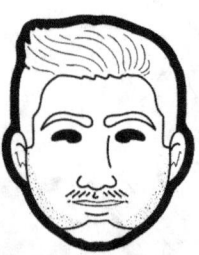 **26**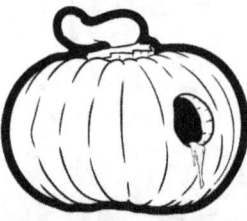

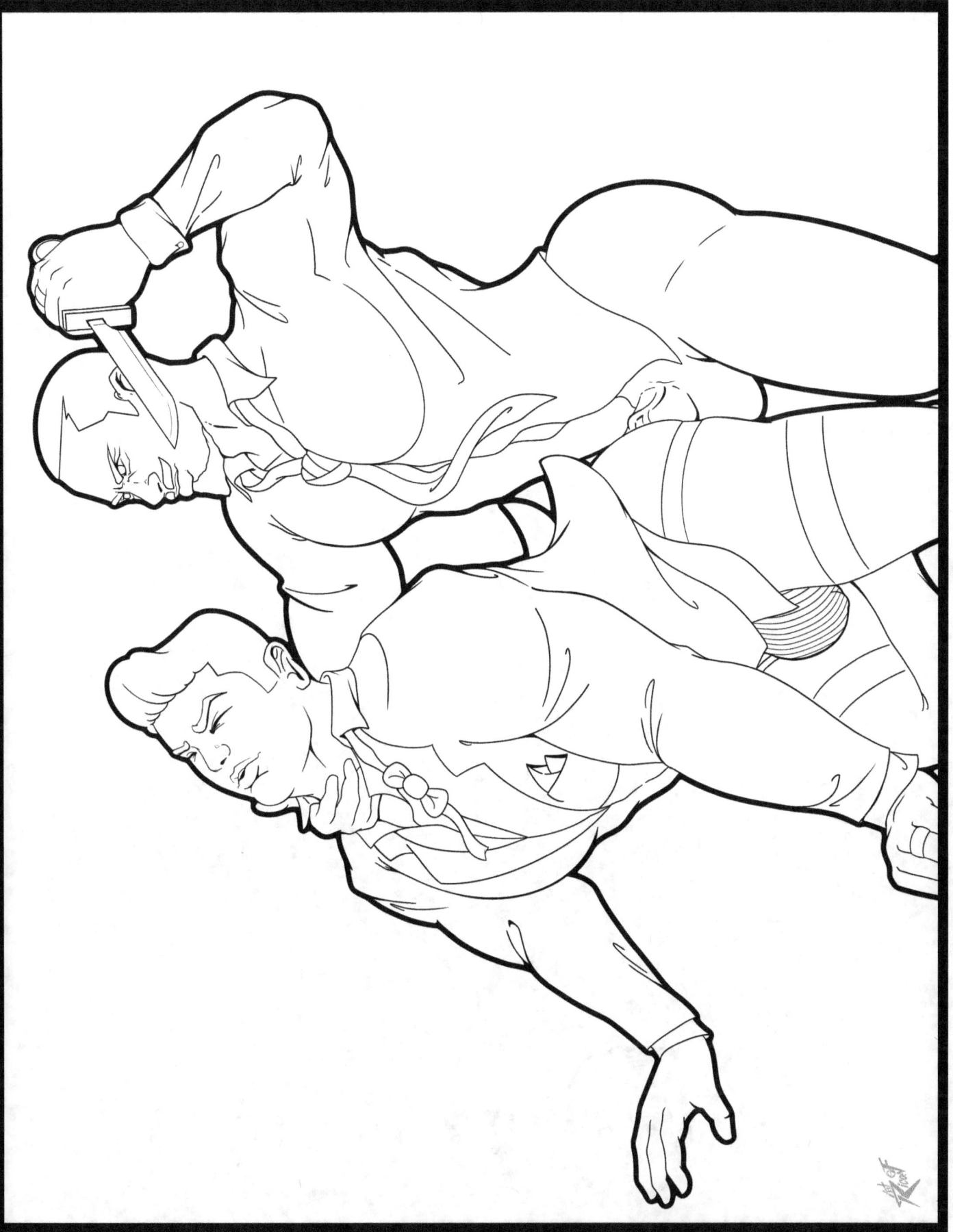

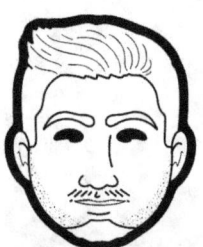 27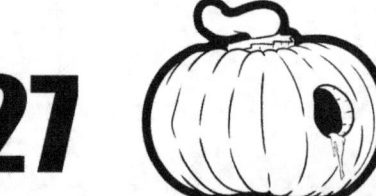

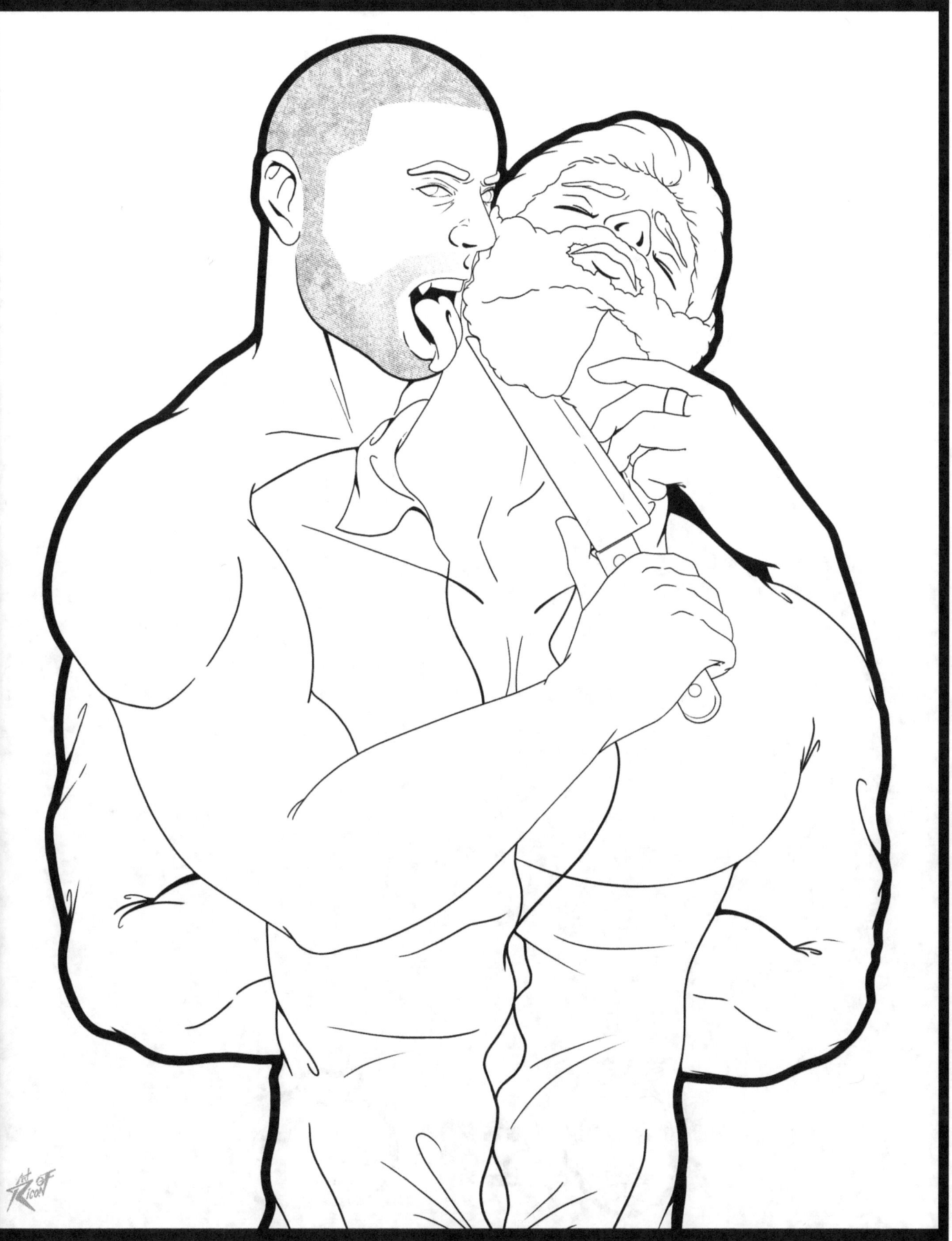

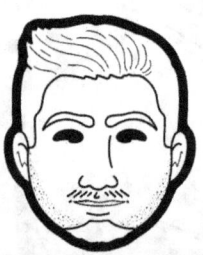 **28**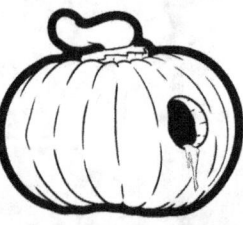

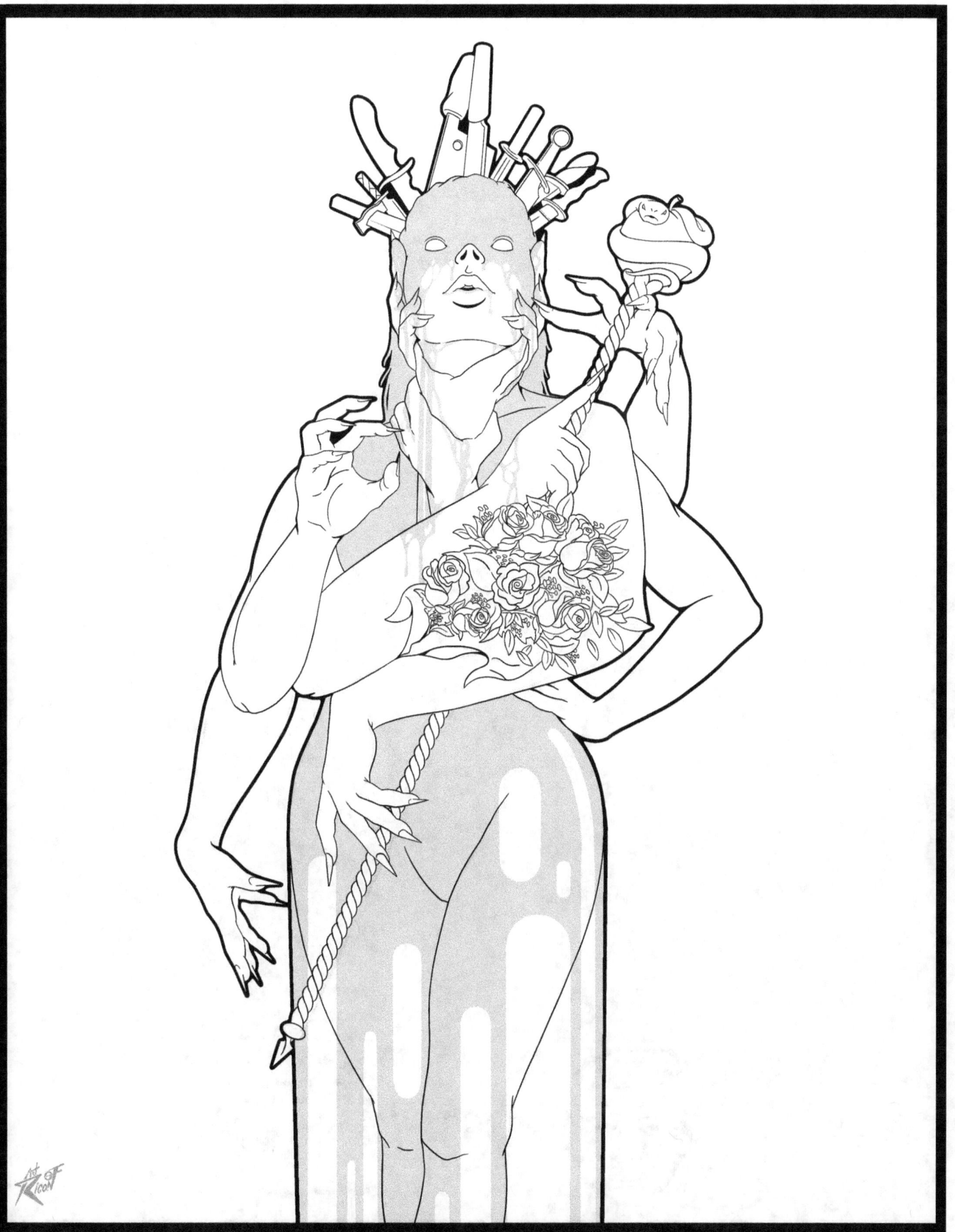

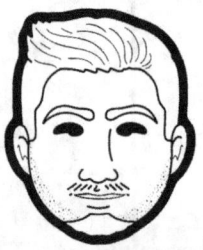 29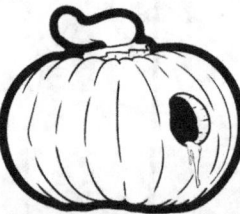

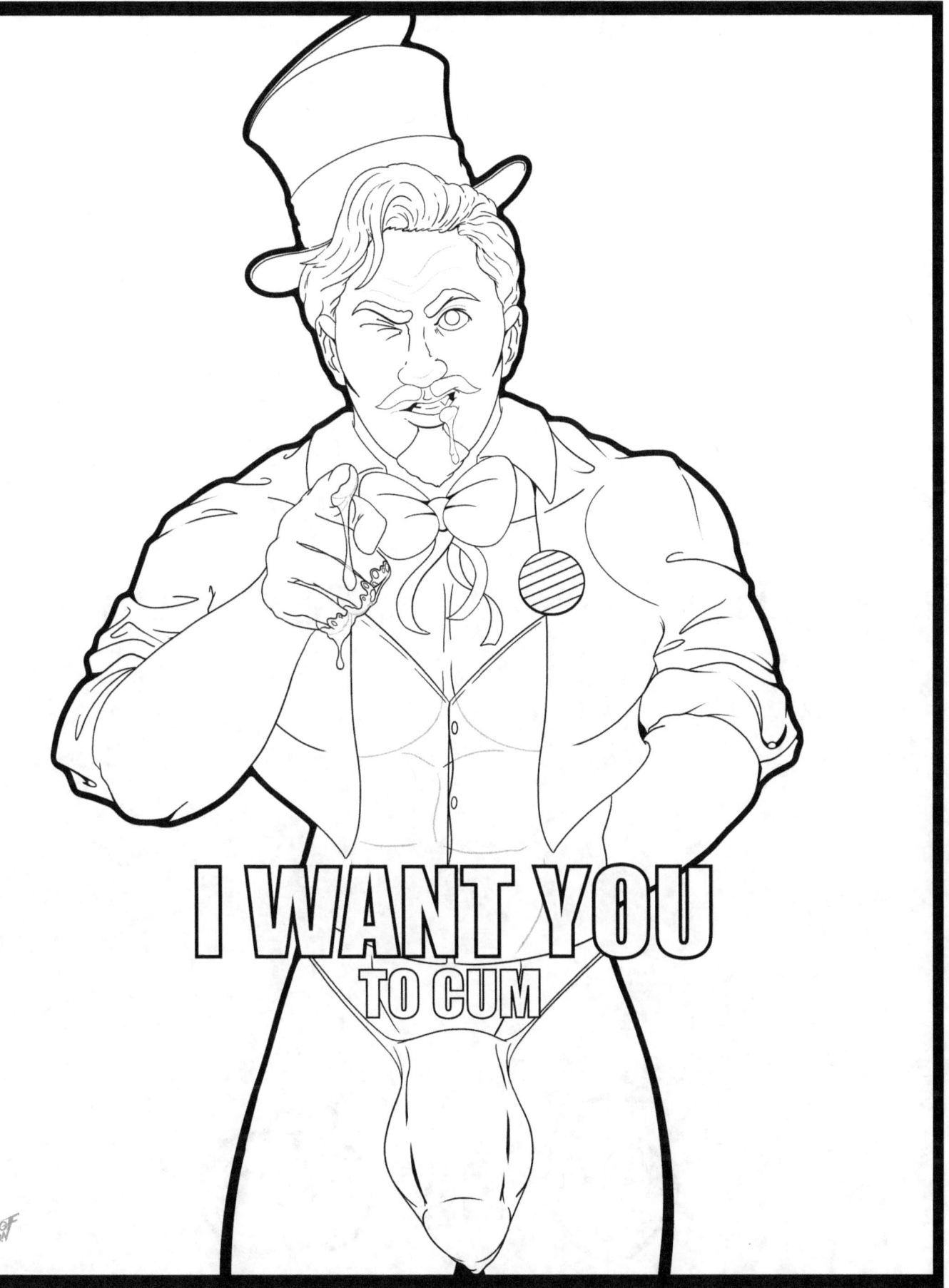

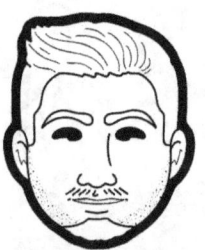

30

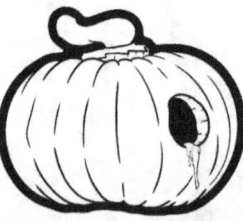

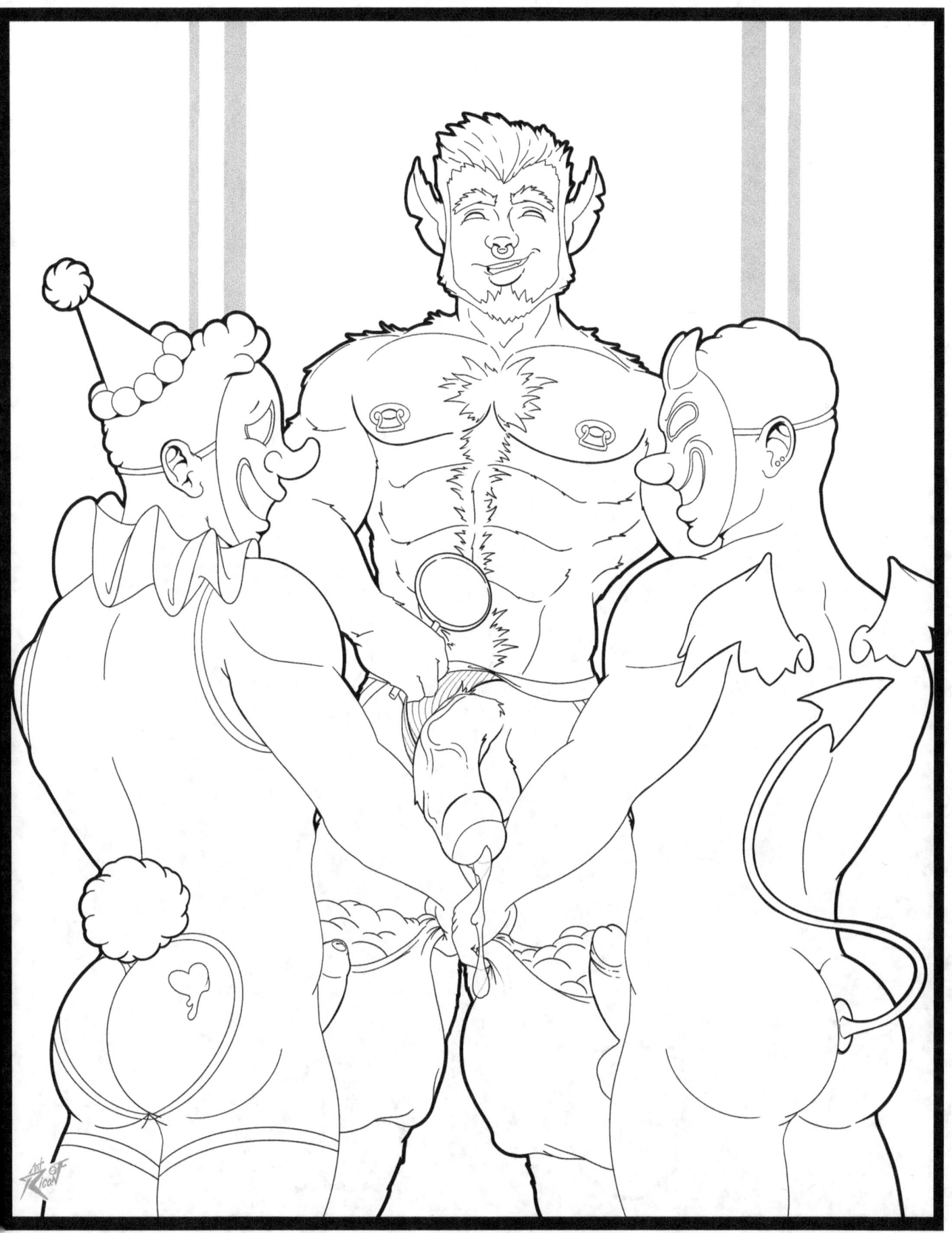

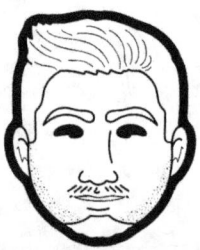 31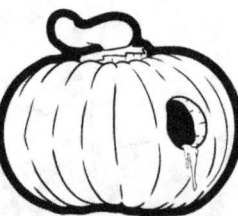

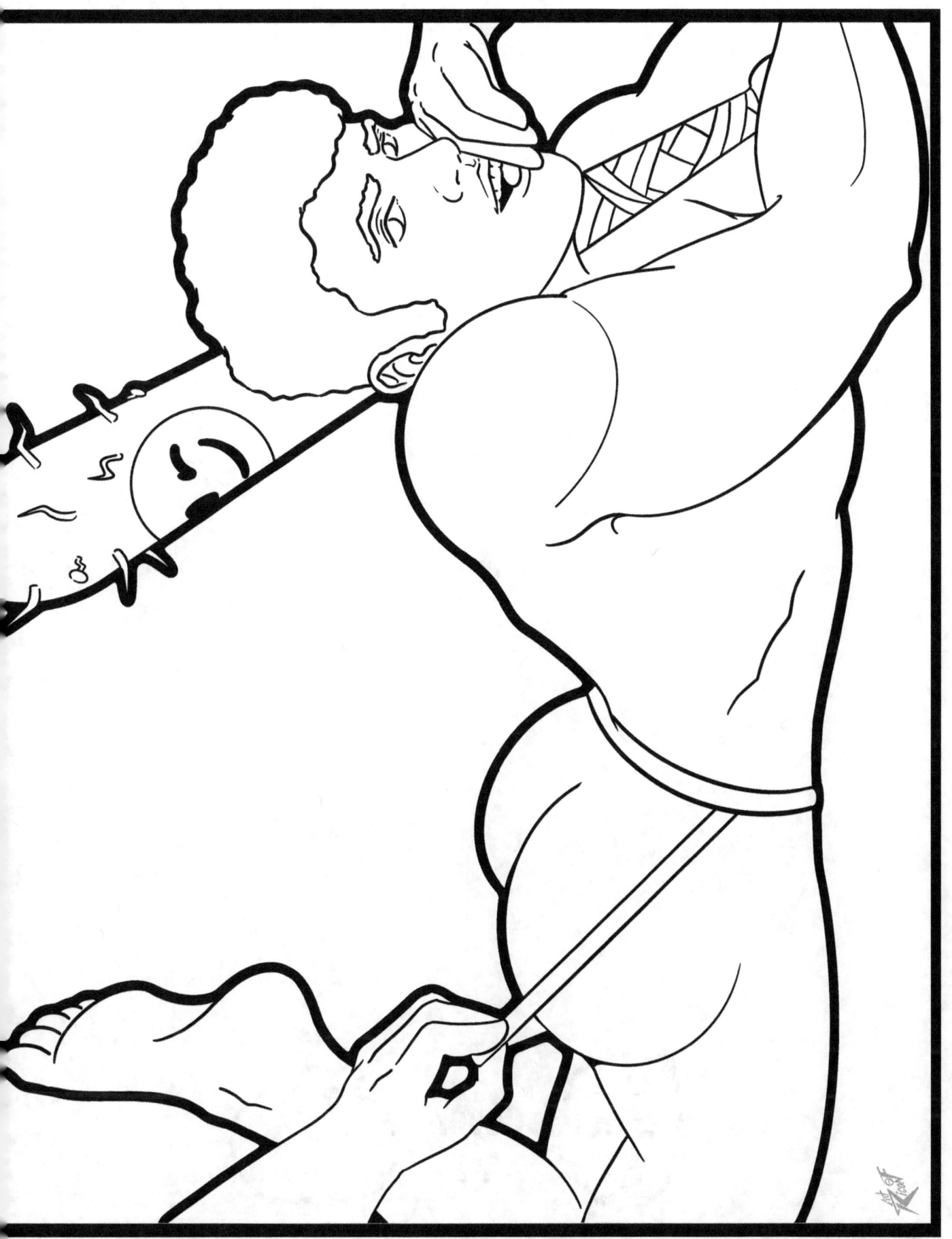

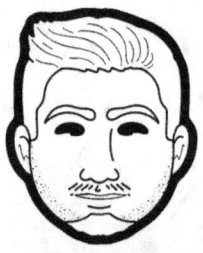

Cover
Art

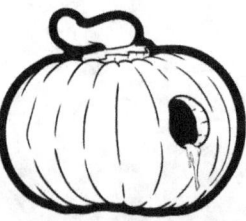